WHAT OTHERS ARE SAYING ABOUT
VORTEX OF THE HOLY SPIRIT

A note from the author: Many people that I know from before and during Superstorm Sandy call me Stan, as that is my first name. It was through the experience of being inside the vortex of the Holy Spirit that God impressed on my heart and my thoughts the suggestion to use my middle name, David, going forward. This is why the name "Stan" is used in the following comments.

It was probably one of the darkest periods in our community's 120-year history. Homes and vehicles were destroyed, electricity and hot water had become rare prized possessions, and people's ruined furniture, memories, and keepsakes were forming mountains on their curbsides. Residents were tired, and many wondered how they were going to clean up and rebuild after a storm named Sandy turned their lives upside down. When it seemed like there was no light and no optimism, rays of hope descended on Little Ferry. A good guy from Indiana, who many in our community would affectionately call "Stan the Man," drove for days to find us after hearing about the problems the storm had caused. With a truck full of food and a grill he set up on Mehrhof Road, Stan not only gave hot food to the hungry residents and volunteers, he also gave us food for thought. He was in many ways a reminder that in this, the greatest nation in the world, we have overcome many obstacles because people of good will open their hearts to others in times of despair and in times of need. Patriotism and kindness don't stop at the borders of red states and blue states; rather, they travel in the hearts of Americans from sea to shining sea. For me personally, he was also a powerful sign that with hard work, unity, and Faith—we would restore and rebuild. I will be forever grateful to Stan.

Mauro Raguseo
Mayor of Little Ferry, New Jersey

Reckless abandon . . . that was the attitude Stan had when he called us on his way out to help the folks affected by Superstorm Sandy. Crazy. Insane. Totally gone. The man we heard talking on the phone was not the friend we had known. He wasn't sure where he was going but he knew Who was sending him, and that was enough. We prayed for both Stan and Susan. Later, the story we heard sounded absolutely nuts, but there was a truth and a contagious enthusiasm that compelled us to listen. As we did, we heard an amazing story of adventure and risk—and what happens when one man takes God seriously. As you meet the people and hear what happened, perhaps you will agree with us that maybe he wasn't so crazy after all!

Reverend Jeff and Julie Buck
Senior Pastor and Wife
Mt. Auburn United Methodist Church
Greenwood, Indiana

Stan Gregory shares the lessons he learned when the Holy Spirit ignited his heart and began to move through him to meet the needs of people affected by Superstorm Sandy. For people he had never met, God placed in his heart a deep fire of love that would not let him go. This unforgettable story will set a fire burning in your own heart to experience God's presence, power, and love as though for the first time. This is an important book for all whose Christianity has become still and sterile. May the 'vortex' of the Spirit move in those who read this book.

Lovingly, but forcefully, Stan calls us, the people of God, to look in the mirror, to repent of all our futile attempts to do the work of the Holy Spirit on our own power, and to get back on our knees where we belong. Only then will God supernaturally move us to accomplish His plan for our ministries and lives. Be prepared to be greatly challenged. You can be sure that reading this book will change you so that the WIND of God will place you in the vortex of Holy Spirit power. Being able to 'pastor' Stan as he experienced the vortex of the Spirit in his life is one of the great privileges of being called into pastoral/shepherding ministry and service. Get ready to feel the Spirit blow across your life!

Steve Beutler
Lead Pastor
Methodist Temple
Evansville, Indiana

At Leadership Evansville, our mission is "Diverse Servant Leaders Transforming Community."

What a pleasure to write about Stan and his incredible passion for helping others. Through his work, he is practicing servant leadership and transforming the lives of countless others.

Servant leadership is the easiest to teach when you can tell a story or use an example of someone who exemplifies the practice. Stan is an incredible example of servant leadership by modeling loving, caring leadership—Stan is more interested in others than himself!

After Superstorm Sandy, he became aware of a need and was moved to action. He did not wait to find out if he was supposed to do it, if he could do it, or even if he was allowed to do it. The need was to feed people after a disaster. He applied caring common sense, and he took it upon himself to load up a grill, buy some food, and go to where the people needed it! Brilliant, gutsy, determined, and loving. In addition, he listened to stories and brought hope and a hot meal!

Stan's actions have made such a profound difference that he became one of the recipients of our Celebration of Leadership

Award. I believe Stan's work has inspired many others to act and lead through his example.

I am honored to know Stan and so proud of the work he does. I know that he has touched hundreds if not thousands of lives through just being willing to give of himself, take the time to do the commonsense next right thing, and truly care and share—especially when people have faced so many difficulties.

Lynn Miller-Pease
Executive Director, Leadership Evansville
Evansville, Indiana

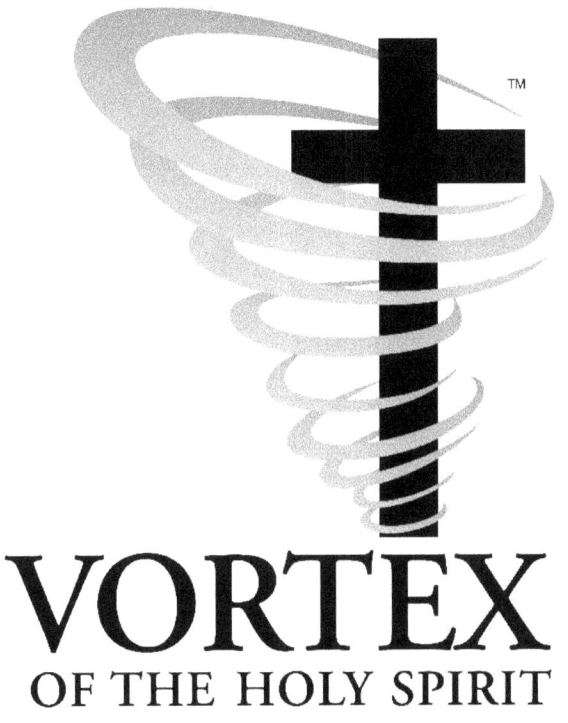

VORTEX
OF THE HOLY SPIRIT

**Finding Supernatural Love
After Superstorm Sandy**

A TRUE STORY

DAVID GREGORY

VORTEX OF THE HOLY SPIRIT
FINDING SUPERNATURAL LOVE AFTER SUPERSTORM SANDY

Copyright © 2015 David Gregory

All rights reserved. No part of this book may be reproduced, stored in a retrieval system, or transmitted in any form or by any means—electronic, mechanical, photocopying, recording, scanning, or other—except for brief quotations in critical reviews or articles, without prior written permission from the author.

Credits
Editor and Designer: Susan Wedeking Gregory
Copy Editor: Dana Monroe Samson

Published in Evansville, Indiana, by Vortex Publishing

Scripture quotations marked NIV are taken from the Holy Bible, New International Version®, NIV®. Copyright © 1973, 1978, 1984, 2011 by Biblica, Inc.™ Used by permission. All rights reserved worldwide.

Scripture quotations marked NLT are taken from the Holy Bible, New Living Translation, copyright © 1996, 2004, 2007, 2013 by Tyndale House Foundation. Used by permission of Tyndale House Publishers, Inc., Carol Stream, Illinois 60188. All rights reserved.

Scripture quotations marked KJV are from the King James Version of the Bible.

ISBN 978-0-9966959-0-9 (Paperback)

Printed in the United States of America

DEDICATION

For you who have experienced a "Superstorm Sandy,"
whether an actual storm or something else
that blew through your life . . .
there is hope.

For you who are ready to get outside of your comfort zone
and move in a new direction . . .
now is the time.

For you who are willing to allow the love
of our Father, the grace from Christ,
and the power of the Holy Spirit
to guide your life . . .
God is there.

CONTENTS

Introduction i

PART ONE

1. A Discomforting Prayer 1
2. Superstorm Sandy Strikes 3
3. Lost in New York 21
4. Arrival in Little Ferry 27
5. Miracles on Mehrhof 37
6. The Journey Home 83
7. The Return Trip 97

PART TWO

8. Anatomy of Vortex of the Holy Spirit 123
9. A Merry-Go-Round Model of the Vortex 129
10. Who Is the Holy Spirit Anyway? 133
11. The Holy Spirit Throughout History 137
12. The Holy Spirit Today:
    Fifty Ways the Holy Spirit Works in Our Lives 143
13. Love Makes the World Go 'Round 157
14. Four Steps of Forgiveness 163
15. Your Story Is Waiting to Be Written 165

Vortex Acknowledgements 167

INTRODUCTION

Have you ever watched the news covering a natural disaster? As you observe the destruction and devastation, you suddenly realize that you haven't moved for several minutes. This happened to me as Superstorm Sandy made landfall and changed thousands of lives. I didn't know it was going to change my life too.

As damage reports kept coming in, I felt an unexplainable and overwhelming need to help. If you've ever felt like this, then I invite you to go with me on a trip to provide food to victims of the storm. The truck is filled with gas and loaded with a grill, meat, and other supplies. From Southwest Indiana we're heading to the East Coast, and it's time to leave. So hop in, buckle up, and I'll fill you in on the details as we go.

PART ONE

A DISCOMFORTING PRAYER

It all started on a Sunday morning in the early fall of 2012. As we usually did, my wife, Susan, and I attended the 8:30 a.m. service at Methodist Temple in Evansville, Indiana. The associate pastor, Chris Neikirk, was delivering the message that morning. When he closed the service with a benediction, he asked God to encourage us to act for the needs of others, to move us out of our comfort zones.

His final words—sounding more like a plea—were, "Please make us uncomfortable and keep us there so that we might see the needs of others in a different way." From the moment I heard those words, there was an unsettling feeling that I took with me.

The service concluded, and the beautiful German pipe organ began to play the postlude. As on most Sundays, a small group of people gathered near the front of the sanctuary to experience the full effect of the music and the powerful sound the instrument could deliver. While the final notes lingered in the sanctuary, everyone broke into an enthusiastic applause in appreciation and reverence for the beauty of the moment.

Susan and I were sitting in the balcony, and we made our way to the side door of the church to leave. When we walked outside, I asked her about the benediction. "Did you pay attention to the final prayer that Pastor Chris gave?" She said she did and asked why. I answered, "I have heard many prayers in my life, but none have included a request for God to make us uncomfortable, to move us out of our comfort zones. Why would any minister want us to be uncomfortable? Do you think something is wrong with him?"

Always the voice of reason, she commented, "He probably just wants us to be more compassionate and sensitive to the needs of others."

I became aware that my heart was beating faster and my breathing was accelerated. I was clearly not comfortable about a prayer asking God to make us uncomfortable. The feeling of discomfort began to subside as I told myself that it was just a prayer and I didn't need to get upset about it. Even so, Pastor Chris's words stuck with me, and I couldn't get the prayer out of my mind the rest of the day. I didn't realize that I had just gotten a sample dose of being "outside the comfort zone."

Pastor Chris was in the early part of his ministry having come from the world of sales and banquet services. He described his calling to the ministry as a distinct message that he had heard. He joined the pastoral team at Methodist Temple while he was attending seminary. His benediction prayer that morning was one that I will never forget.

SUPERSTORM SANDY STRIKES

Now spin the calendar forward a couple of months to the evening of Monday, October 29, 2012. Susan and I watched the news for hours as Hurricane Sandy made its way up the eastern coast of the United States. It had started a few days earlier as a tropical storm in the Caribbean and was picking up strength, size, and intensity as it moved steadily up the coastline, ultimately growing to more than 800 miles wide.

Compounding the situation, the atmospheric conditions in New England that night were highly unusual. There was a cold front moving in from the west, and the Atlantic Ocean was at high tide—bolstered by a full moon. The resulting gale force winds and storm surges created a stirring cauldron that transformed Hurricane Sandy into a superstorm.

A satellite image taken Monday, October 29, 2012, shows Hurricane Sandy off the Mid-Atlantic coastline moving toward the north.

We watched in disbelief and horror as the power of the wind and water took its toll in New York and New Jersey. A crane that was being used in a Midtown luxury apartment construction project had broken, and the boom was hanging 1,000 feet over 57th Street. We wondered if it would hold or if it would snap and come crashing into the street below. Thankfully, it held. Streets were flooded as the seawater poured inland. Fires popped up as gas lines broke.

Breezy Point, a closely knit community of firefighters and first responders in Queens, was engulfed in flames—and at the same time was surrounded by rising water that kept rescuers from being able to reach the area. The potential for loss of life and damage to property was hard to imagine.

Sleeping was a challenge for Susan and me that night as we both kept thinking about the storm.

I woke up at 4:15 the next morning, and my first thought was to see what else had happened during the night. I went downstairs to turn on the television to the news channel. The first image I saw was the famous Coney Island roller coaster lying submerged in the ocean with destruction all around it. The bad news kept coming.

I was becoming so uncomfortable with the images on television that I got up from the sofa and continued watching the news while walking in circles around the living room. I soon realized that my heart was beating faster and my breathing was accelerated. I was growing more uncomfortable with each passing minute. It was as though I began to experience the pain and suffering of the people who had been impacted by the storm. I didn't know anyone in the Northeast, yet as I thought about the people there, their pain seemed to become my pain.

I continued to pace around the room and suddenly heard Susan say, "Why are you walking in circles around the sofa?" I said, "Look what happened. Look at the devastation!" She stood motionless as I kept circling the sofas. She said, "It is horrible, but what do you want to do about it?" (That was a strange question . . . Why would she suppose I could do anything about it?) But without thinking about it I said, "They have no electricity and probably won't have it for days. They are going to be hungry. I could take my grill, get some food, and go cook for them. They will smell the smoke in the air and come and get something to eat."

I was so surprised to hear what came out of my mouth that I wasn't sure why I had said it. I expected a logical reaction from her that would have ended the conversation right then and there. We have been together for over twenty years, and I was almost certain that her response would be something like, "Well, that may be a great idea—why don't we think about it and talk around noon and maybe decide this evening after I get home from work."

But no, that is not what she said at all. Her response to me was as immediate as my answer to her question. She said,

"THEN I SUGGEST YOU GET YOUR BAGS PACKED!"

I couldn't believe what I had heard come out of her mouth. There was a certain inflection in her voice that caused me to take heed. She meant it. She then arose to go upstairs. I said, "Wait a minute! Where are you going?" She responded in the most casual way, saying, "I am going to take a shower and get ready for work." Unbelievable! She just affirmed and confirmed that I should head to the East Coast and find some people who need help.

Susan left the room without saying another word. Now what? I started to have my own rising tide of emotions as I began to question what we both had just said. What was I thinking? I don't know anyone on the East Coast. Where will I go? More importantly, why do I feel compelled to go help? I am not an emergency responder. Can one guy with a grill really make a difference?

Although I was filled with questions, the thought of going was growing by the minute. I was self-employed and figured I could rearrange my schedule to be gone for the next few days.

My heart was pounding, and I was breathing as though I had been jogging for thirty minutes as the *idea* of going to help and the *reality* of what it would take to get ready to leave began to sink in. Somehow, during these moments of uncertainty, everything changed.

It seemed like an incredible energy had just filled the room. It felt heavy and I found it difficult to move. What was **"IT"** that could cause this surreal moment? Inside these motionless moments of introspection, I began to experience a slight spinning sensation. What would cause me to feel this way?

Amid this feeling, I suddenly realized that Susan was standing in the room again. She had decided to take the day off to gather supplies and help me get ready to go. We divided our efforts, and she went her way and I went mine. We planned to meet back at our home later in the day.

NO MORE "WHY AM I DOING THIS?" IT'S GAME ON.

My first thought was to see if someone could go with me. For many reasons, it would be better not to be alone. A companion could help with the driving and help determine where we should go and what we should do, and we could keep each other company. It was bound to be a long drive.

I immediately thought of my friend Bruce who loved to help with just about anything disaster-relief-related. We had worked together on an aid project in the months following Hurricane Katrina, but neither of us had been involved in relief efforts in the days that immediately followed a natural disaster.

Bruce is a school teacher, so it would be a longshot for him to be able to go, but I called him anyway and told him about my plan. He said he would love to go but had commitments at school, so he had to decline. He said he hoped to be able to get up there soon.

After mentally running through the rather short list of other people who might be able to go and crossing them off for one reason or another, I realized that I would be going by myself. It wasn't my preference, but my determination to go was growing.

I was eager to get started but felt uncertain about what to do next. I was sure of only one thing and that was that I needed to see Pastor Steve, the senior pastor from church, before I did anything. I needed his wisdom, his discerning counsel, and mainly his friendship. Pastor Steve and I are close in age, and in the past, we had shared a few personal stories. But now, his day was about to change. I called the church office to make an appointment. He said I could come right over.

As I walked to my car, the world around me seemed energizing. Birds were singing their solos and right on pitch. The deer were at peace with several does eating grass in the field next to our house. A hint of fall was in the air, bringing with it relief from the oppressive Southern Indiana humidity. Every sound, sight, and smell seemed to be a reminder of nature at its finest. This was in direct contrast to how I was feeling inside. The complexity of the moment strengthened my need to get to Pastor Steve's office ASAP.

I arrived at the church, and he was standing at his office door patiently waiting on me to come in. He had a cheery smile and seemed excited to know all about what was going on and eager to assist me in any way possible. I told him what had happened the night before and, more importantly, what had happened from 4:15 a.m. until then. My first question to him was, "Do you think I'm crazy?" The more times I questioned my sanity, the more scripture he offered to support what I was getting ready to do.

He explained the mystery of God's intervention by using scripture that calls us to serve and become servants. We discussed other aspects of the upcoming trip, but faith and prayer would be the most important tools to overcome all adversities. He then moved us to a time of prayer in which he asked for a special blessing for all of the steps necessary to complete God's will and His plan. He also offered resources from the church's disaster relief fund to help make the trip possible. The meeting gave me insight and the fortification to keep going.

I left the church and went to Sam's Club to purchase a small tailgate grill and cooler. I then headed home to put together the equipment I might need. I didn't know what conditions I would encounter, so I took a little of everything including hand tools, a chain saw, shovels, gloves, trash bags, jumper cables, rope, coveralls, and a sleeping bag and pillow. I wanted to be prepared and packed it all in the back of our pickup truck.

As I walked into our home, the television was on and the news was nonstop coverage of Superstorm Sandy. The damage sustained in the state of New Jersey continued to be covered extensively. It began to make sense to me that New Jersey was the logical place to set up the grill and serve food. I was not concerned about any aspect of getting there because my cell phone could literally tell me every turn to make. The only slight problem was that New Jersey has 8,722 square miles of land mass, and I had no idea which seventy square feet I should be parked in. Susan got home shortly after I did and said that she wanted me to take three extra five-gallon gas cans because gasoline was being rationed in the New Jersey and New York areas and she did not want me to be stranded.

Gathering supplies and packing the truck had taken most of the day, and I was starting to get tired. The emotions of the day were swirling in my head, and my ability to concentrate was fading. I caught myself stopping and staring out the window with no concept of time. Susan sensed that I was struggling with everything, so she told me that it might be better to get a decent night's sleep and leave tomorrow. I agreed without comment and decided to enjoy one more night in my own bed. That evening, I couldn't watch any more television—the continual coverage of the devastation was more than I could take.

The next morning, I was in the shower early with one thing on my mind, and that was leaving. I had thought through as many variables as possible and determined that whatever I didn't know, I would figure out on the way. I had one important call left to make, and that was to the local meat retailer Dewig Meats and my friends Janet and Tom who own it.

Susan and I were both rushing around, but before she left for work, she brought a note pad and asked me to write some things down:

1. Don't leave without fifteen extra gallons of gas
2. Concentrate on my driving
3. Don't drive when I get sleepy
4. Take some pictures
5. Call your wife

She walked across the room and took my chin and lifted it up and said, "Look at me." I said, "Okay, what?" She said, "I have to leave, and I probably won't see you for a while. Please figure out where you are going as soon as possible and let me know. Remember to call Janet, and don't take any chances on driving if you get sleepy. I don't care where you are—I want you to stop and get a motel if you get sleepy. Now, give me a hug and a kiss." With that she was off to work, and I was out the door to load more supplies.

A short time later, I called Janet and told her what I was doing in response to Superstorm Sandy and asked if they might be willing to donate some food that I could take with me. I didn't have to say much because she was so receptive to what I was doing. She said, "We will get you fixed right up." I told her that I was leaving later that morning, and she said they would have everything ready.

I finished packing and headed to Haubstadt, a small town about fifteen miles north of Evansville. I walked through the door at Dewig's and was treated like a family member. They donated two large boxes of frozen meat, one each of center cut pork chops and bratwurst. Tom and Janet have servants' hearts and have proven it over and over throughout the years with their generosity to local causes. I loaded up the meat, gave them a hug, and said goodbye.

Tom and Janet Dewig provided a generous food donation for the trip.

HOUSTON: WE HAVE A LIFTOFF

I was finally and officially on the road. When I made it to the clover leaf to head east on I-64, I rolled the window down, stuck my hand in the air with my thumb extended and laid on the horn. I was loaded with supplies and fired up. A passing truck driver honked his horn and waved. He somehow connected with me and signaled that he approved. This moment was a kind of feeling beyond happiness and briefly reminded me of a talk from Pastor Steve teaching us that "joy is divine, and happiness is a human emotion." Joy is "God given" and eternal. Happiness depends on other circumstances. I didn't care who saw my joyful moment, it was totally exhilarating!

There was no more getting ready to leave, which already had taken a day and a half. I was looking forward to finding a spot to set up the grill and get started cooking. Grilling out is fun. I love it and learned how to cook on a grill before I was a teenager. Everyone seems to enjoy smelling the smoke (except maybe vegetarians, of which Susan is one).

My moment of elation was quickly replaced with the reality that I did not know where I was going. I was heading northeast and expected to end up somewhere in New Jersey. That left me about fifteen hours to figure out where in the state to go.

Before long, I was north of Louisville on I-71 and crossing the Ohio River. As I glanced at the beauty of the river, feelings of doubt were creeping back into my thoughts. "What am I doing, and why am I doing this?"

As I continued getting closer to New Jersey, my doubts grew stronger. I would oscillate toward doubt and suddenly get a dose of strength in faith. This was an emotional tug of war between myself and me. If I were dancing, it was three steps forward and one step backwards.

Christianetically (not in Webster's) speaking, when I leaned on my own understanding, I felt emotional turbulence fueled by doubt and confusion. (For example: You won't know where to go . . . You won't find anyone who wants food that is cooked in a truck . . . You will probably get arrested for disturbing the peace.) When I stopped trying to understand, there was CALMNESS. (For example: Quit trying to understand why you are doing this . . . You can make a difference . . . Keep going . . . Think of the people who are without electricity and are missing meals.) These messages gave me peace, and I sensed—or thought that I sensed—a Presence in the seat next to me. Even if I was pretending the Presence was in the seat, it was what I needed to get through the next ten hours of driving.

My brain seemed to become a "control tower" of doubt, and my heart seemed to become a "control tower" of reason. Brain messages: "You have lost your mind, and you are clueless. You don't know where you are going, so turn around and go home." Heart messages: "You are going to help someone. You will find where you are supposed to be, so keep driving."

My phone and charger stayed plugged in because I remained in conversations for hours to find reinforcement for what I was doing, check my sanity, and check with Mike, a friend from high school and now a professional truck driver, for directions. He knows most of the roads and truck stops in this country by heart. His network of driver friends could tell you if there was a frog jumping across the interstate and at which mile marker it was taking place.

When I told him what I was doing, and because of our forty-year friendship, he said, "You are taking a grill to Jersey? You are going to grill out for people you don't even know? Have I told you lately that you are an idiot?"

His casual conversation was refreshing amid my own confusion. He gave me two optional routes depending on which food buffet I might be interested in. I told him that I was not on vacation and it didn't matter who had barbequed versus fried chicken on the menu—just get me to Jersey the quickest way and avoid road construction if possible. His initial plan was to route me through Philadelphia, but he said he would make some calls to friends who had just been through the area and get back with me.

A short time later, as I turned east out of Columbus, Ohio, I decided to call our good friend and former pastor Jeff and his wife, Julie, who were now serving at Emmanuel Methodist Church in Noblesville, Indiana. Jeff answered, and I asked if he had some time to talk. Jeff and Julie were on a trip heading somewhere, so the timing of the call was excellent.

Susan and I had met Jeff and Julie when Jeff was appointed to Old North United Methodist Church in Evansville, which we attended several years ago. They have four children, and we had spent several close years with them and their family when they lived in town. After Jeff was appointed to Noblesville, we kept in touch but rarely saw them.

We quickly got caught up on the latest family activities and then started talking about the damage from Superstorm Sandy and, more importantly, Susan's and my response to the victims of the storm. I reviewed the entire story that led me to where I was. He suddenly interrupted his silence with a sound of snickering or muffled giggling. (He was probably putting his hand over the phone to keep me from hearing it.) I said, "Jeff, are you laughing?" He replied, "I am just smiling, but this is a great story. I'm sorry, please go on."

Jeff knew the right things to say for any situation. At this point, my biggest issue was not leaving my comfort zone—which I had already done—it was the challenge of maintaining my sanity to effectively help with relief for the victims of the storm. Jeff spoke about me driving by myself but assured me that I was not alone. He said that I would recognize the signs to put me in the right place at the right time.

Suddenly, Julie interrupted Jeff and asked to speak with me. She said, "We love you and we support your efforts, but you have no idea what you are getting into and you don't know who or what you will be dealing with." I instantly felt a cautious, yet supportive, energy in her voice. "You need to know that we are here for you any moment during your trip. We will have our phones with us, and we want you to call us with any problems 24/7." Julie gave the phone back to Jeff, and we wrapped up our call.

The energy from the call was overwhelming, and I now felt a slight spinning motion again. Our conversation was what I needed and when I needed it. They had no idea what had happened to get me where I was, but they knew that Susan and I were both involved. There was solace in the fact that there would be two "angels" available for my intercession henceforth. I didn't think that we would talk again soon, but I was wrong.

My next task was to figure out where I could go to set up my grill. I was hoping to connect with a Methodist church in the area because churches are often the sites of disaster relief efforts. I thought both victims and volunteers would be coming to churches to find help. I spent the next two hours trying to contact Methodist church offices along the Jersey Shore and must have made twenty calls, but no one answered. I included district superintendents' offices in the mix of calls and still had no luck at finding anyone who could answer their phone.

Another idea was to call one of the major relief organizations and ask if they knew where centers were being set up in the Jersey area. I was able to reach someone, and the person could not have been nicer or more discouraging. She said that teams had not even attempted making evaluations in the area because of the enormity of damage. She suggested going back home and returning at another time when "things were more settled."

My response was, "I am halfway there, and 'I am settled' in the fact that I am bringing them hot food. I will not be turning around and will find people to feed." I politely thanked her and ended the call. I was now fueled with absolute determination to get there. I looked down and my speed had increased to eighty-five miles per hour, which I immediately corrected.

My perceived "co-pilot" seemed to be questioning me by asking, "Why do you continue to seek validation from people? You won't listen, and you don't pay attention. Be still and know that I will show you what you need to know." At this point, I did not hear a voice distinctly but did feel the thought or received the thought.

I began to feel tired, and suddenly my phone rang and it was Susan. Her first words were always, "How's it going?" My answer was enough for her to know that I was getting sleepy, so she kindly reminded me of the directive to get a motel when I got sleepy. I promised to find something in the area around Washington, Pennsylvania, which was not far away. I found the exit, got a room for the night, and unloaded some clothes. With my last ounce of energy, I headed to Home Depot to get another five-gallon plastic container for extra gas. I met a manager who said that Sandy had caused the biggest shortage of supplies that he had ever seen. They ran out of generators first and plastic gas containers second. He was located nearly four hours west of Philadelphia and ran out of gas cans? This was my first personal contact with the storm's impact. There would be much more.

Back at the motel, I parked the truck where it was visible from my room, but I was too exhausted to stay awake and watch for thieves. I trusted that the food inside the cooler would be there in the morning.

I awakened early the following day and decided to check the cooler first. Everything was in its rightful place. I found coffee and breakfast nearby, and it seemed like every conversation in the restaurant was about the damage from the storm or family members who had not been heard from. Many cell phone towers were down, affecting a huge coverage area for those trying to communicate. I tried to ignore the conversations and worked on my route to the Jersey Shore.

I soon realized that Philadelphia would be my last city for supplies. Philly had a Sam's Club, so I worked on a list of things still needed. I sat there and thought: How do you plan for several meals to grill, but you don't know where you are going or how many people are going to show up? As I paid the bill for breakfast, I neatly folded the list and threw it in the trash can beside the counter. I figured that when I got to Sam's, the list would come to me.

SIGNS OF A NATIONAL RESPONSE

I left the restaurant and was on the road again. As I entered the on-ramp of the Interstate, the entire trip took on a different look. Tractors with fifty-three foot trailers loaded with the most enormous electrical generators I had ever seen were moving east bound. Units of the National Guard in Humvees were moving east toward the disaster area. Fire engines, ambulances, and a plethora of industrial equipment were all headed to the East Coast. Everyone would have a job when they got there. There were thousands of people collectively moving toward the assistance of someone else. It felt great to be moving with them in the same direction.

The trip to Philadelphia took about four hours. Sam's Club was an easy exit for ingress and egress off the highway. I went in, grabbed a huge cooler, and proceeded to shop for supplies such as hot dogs, water, plates, napkins, buns, and condiments. I spent about an hour trying to be reasonable with every item and thinking about the possibility of large crowds. While loading the meat into the cooler and buns in the back seat with all of the other items, I asked a lady to take a picture.

With the truck loaded with additional supplies, I was ready to continue the journey.

Things were changing rapidly, and I soon saw a "Welcome to New Jersey" sign. The highway was a beautiful road that headed toward the beach area, which was about ninety minutes away. It was the first time that I had driven to New Jersey. After entering the state, I noticed that not one stop light was operating. It added to the exhilaration at every crossroad. To be extra safe, for any car approaching an intersection with a stoplight, I would stop and wait to let it pass. I still didn't know where I was going, but the beach area seemed like a good place to start.

I finally made it to a quaint, slightly populated area outside Asbury Park. It was getting late, and I did not have two hours of daylight left to search for a place to set up the grill. I wanted to see the beach and consider setting up there if I could. But there was so much water in the town that the access road to the beach was impassable. I stayed more inland on a main highway rather than attempting any other beach access.

Water was everywhere! Storefronts had water submerging the entire sidewalk leading up to them. Roads were visible in one place and not another. I had heard that the army was not allowing people access to the beaches because of all the damage. I was too far inland to see the beach, but the main problem was water and wind damage to the entire area.

Restaurants were closed in some areas and open in others. The idea of grilling yet that day was fading fast. Water was everywhere, and there were not many people anywhere except in the restaurants and hotels that were open. I found a deli-type restaurant and stopped to take a break and eat. I was losing energy and observing the devastation and feeling that the stress of everything had turned into an ache in my neck and shoulders. My phone would ring soon, and the question would be presented, "Are you cooking yet?" That thought sent me out to find churches, any churches.

Everyone seemed to have gone inland to escape the forces of the massive winds. I could not find a church with electricity or people and the daylight was nearly gone, so I began the arduous task of finding a motel. Every motel sign I found in a five-mile radius read, "No Vacancy." Now what do I do? The phone rang, and Susan asked the question about getting set up. I told her that the beach did not look promising and that by driving back to Philly, I would maybe find a hotel and get some sleep. Then I could start searching for the right place to set up on Friday morning.

The sixty-minute trip back was not one that I would wish on anyone. I went through several intersections without stop lights that became close calls with other close calls. I was having trouble staying awake and had no idea where the best place to find a room was. I kept driving until I saw some lights and people and went to several hotels on the east side of Philly. Negotiating on ramps and off ramps in Philadelphia was an act of futility. The same signs were in the windows as out on the beach: "No Vacancy."

I gave up on the thought of getting a room, and the idea of sleeping in the truck was becoming a likelihood, which was not part of my plan—forgetting the fact that I had no plan and now, no hotel. Finally after seeing six or more hotels with no vacancy signs, I found a donut shop. I went inside for my last efforts to better understand my location. I sat with my phone searching the area and calling hotels with no luck at all—and spent over ninety minutes trying to find a room. There were no rooms to find, and 1:30 a.m. turned into 3:00 a.m. very quickly.

So I got back in the truck and decided to go across the street where a huge truck was being unloaded at a furniture store. I made my way across and luckily found a brightly lit area, notwithstanding the fact that it wasn't a tourist rest stop. So, I was in a parking lot area that was well lit but with questionable safety for sleeping. I parked my truck near the delivery vehicle and reclined my seat and closed my eyes. It was not quality rest, but it really helped.

LOST IN NEW YORK

Day Three, Friday, November 2

In a few short hours, the sun was bright, and the parking lot started filling up with cars, so it was time to rock and roll.

Now this was my third time to travel Highway 70, and I was hoping to go back where I had come from the previous night and head north from there. I just wanted something that would feel familiar. The area was called Toms River, New Jersey.

It was a beautiful morning—sunny and cool with the smell of fall. It was the kind when you feel energy in the air, and it's invigorating just to breathe. I was feeling moments of joy and seconds of asking myself, "What are you doing?"

The phone rang, and Susan was checking on me and wanted to know if I had had a restful night. I filled her in, especially about the hotel problem. She was not happy about the hotel situation but impressed upon me that I was on day three. She asked if I knew where I was going, and I told her that I was heading toward north New Jersey. She said that details of my route were unnecessary, but grilling pork chops needed to happen. I gave a grumble and said goodbye.

The incredible wind damage and no electricity in several towns I passed caused me to keep going north. I began to see long lines of people working with plastic gas cans and trying to get their share of rationed gas. Every convenience store and every store along the route was crowded with long lines of people—all trying to get gas. I passed a CNN van with reporters heading to cover the news.

The shortage of gasoline caused a run on gas stations.

I was running out of options going north and needed to get on I-95. Without realizing it, I had merged into the lane for Highway 278. The signs were similar colors. Suddenly, I realized that there was no turning around and that I had merged into a lane leading to Verrazano-Narrows Bridge.

Lanes of traffic were merging, and traffic began to swell. There was absolutely nothing I could do about it—I was going across the bridge. Before long, I was approximately 300 feet above the water and suspended between two 693-foot-tall towers that spanned 4,260 feet. I was doing fine with everything until the traffic stalled about midway across the bridge. There I sat swinging in the air on this double-decker monster of a bridge with six lanes of traffic. I was almost air sick from the elevation, but the beautiful view was awesome.

I was surrounded on the bridge by utility trucks from all over the United States. Disaster relief trucks were everywhere and converging on New York City where I was now headed. It was awesome, and it was American at the same time. A blonde-headed guy, maybe thirty-five, driving beside me yelled at me while I had the window down. I thought he was asking me what time it was, but after lowering the passenger window he said, "What time is happy hour? I see you have the grill to go with it." We talked as we made our way across the bridge. He was from South Carolina and was being followed by five identical trucks from the same company.

Crossing the Verrazano-Narrows Bridge with a view of Manhattan out the window and a steady line of traffic in the rearview mirror.

After exiting the bridge, I went through the southwest tip of Brooklyn. I noticed tall apartment buildings with windows open for fresh air since electricity was not available. Many people were moving around as if in a twilight zone—moving aimlessly as if they didn't know where to go. Others were walking around looking for stores that might be open.

The usual hustle and bustle that I had seen on television was non-existent. I looked up at a five-story apartment building, and an older couple stood and stared out the window while the cat was being held by the wife. Another window on the second floor revealed a student reading or studying a textbook in her window with one leg hanging down moving slowly back and forth. Everyone was just moving slowly about since nobody had electricity.

I continued to travel north and hardly saw a car and rarely saw a taxi. I did notice two young police officers, a man and a woman, walking up the street. The woman appeared to be less than thirty, and the man could have been about thirty five—both seemed to be in absolute peak physical condition. I wanted to speak with them, so I parked the truck on the side of the street proximate to their location and decided to get out.

I walked across the street to say hello and get some information. They seemed to move their hands toward their belts. (I assumed that most people do not hail police in New York for casual conversation very often.) I continued to approach them and then said, "How are you guys?" With one sound of my Southern Indiana accent and tone of voice, they looked at each other and smiled.

We spoke for a few minutes as I explained what I was doing. They looked at me like I was mentally unstable, but I had them giggling in no time. I asked them for their opinions on the worst area to set up the grill to cook. They discussed the answer with each other and then said, "You need to take the tunnel and go back to New Jersey and find a borough called Little Ferry. The entire area sustained tremendous water damage, and that area is where you need to be." They gave me directions to the tunnel. I thanked them and walked back across the street, jumped in the truck, and followed their instructions.

As I approached the tunnel, barricades blocked all of the entrances with police on hand to direct traffic. The tunnel was closed due to the flooding. I asked the best way back to New Jersey. They told me to go north and catch the George Washington Bridge. I would pass a city called Fort Lee, and Little Ferry was west of that.

So I was sitting in New York . . . I needed to be across the bridge on the Jersey side . . . I felt certain that my phone was about to ring with a familiar inquiry about the progress of grilling food. At least I now had a destination, and somehow I was going to fire up the grill and go door-to-door, if I had to, this day. However, I needed to be in the right state.

I was told to take 9A and stay on it until I saw the bridge. The drive faced the Hudson River. I enjoyed the scenery, but it was odd with no electricity or lights and very little traffic. I was driving north toward the bridge, and the sight of century-old homes with beautiful white picket fences and curved turrets was very interesting. The phone started to ring, and my first thought was: it's her and I am dead. I looked at the phone, and it was my son Brandon. I thought the timing was unusual, but I wanted to answer. We had spoken earlier in the week, and he knew that I was in the New York City area. He did not know that I was heading to the George Washington Bridge to cross over to New Jersey.

He said, "Hey Dad, I was just wondering—where are you right now?" I said that I was heading north toward the George Washington Bridge. He then wanted the exact cross streets, so I gave him Riverside Drive and 102nd Street.

He placed me on hold a short time and came back on the phone and said, "I know you are probably busy, but there is a car dealership within minutes of the bridge in a city called Ft. Lee, New Jersey. I have been watching the price go down on this one vehicle, and I am really curious what it looks like. Could you stop by and quickly look at it and maybe test drive it?" There was a huge pause in the conversation, and I felt a voice (like my late mother) saying: "Do not tell him no. You are his dad. He hardly ever calls you and asks for a favor—this won't take you twenty minutes." Suddenly every fiber of what I was trying to do collided with every fiber I have as a father, and I replied, "Okay, this will have to be brief because Susan is about to call, and I am supposed to be feeding people. I am in the wrong state, and she is going to kill me if she finds this out, but yes, I will." He replied, "Okay, I'm really going to help you out. When you get on the George Washington Bridge, call me and I'll walk you through the directions to the dealership." I said, "If the dealership is busy and I can't get any service, I'll have to leave. I will not have time to wait." He agreed to that.

As I approached the Ft. Lee exit, I called Bran and he was prepared with a map, so he began to give directions. After a number of attempts, I was able to locate the building and pull into the parking lot. The dealership was open, and I was greeted by a very nice sales representative. He found the keys to the vehicle that I was supposed to be driving and asked a lady who worked in the office to find and print a map to Little Ferry. He quickly showed me the vehicle, and we drove it. They handed me the map, and the entire process only took about thirty minutes. I reported my assessment on the vehicle to Bran, and map in hand, headed toward my destination. I knew that Little Ferry was not far away. Ft. Lee had several trees twisted and lying near the streets. Some siding was blown about, and shingles were missing on several roofs. There was obvious wind damage, but their topography and elevation seemed to have protected them from much of the severe water damage.

What I didn't know then was that what seemed like a setback was actually an integral part of the chain of events that was about to take place. Without the delay, this story may not have been written.

ARRIVAL IN LITTLE FERRY

Friday, 3:00 p.m.

I took Highway 46 westbound and began to see more evidence of wind and water damage such as no electricity and no stop lights working. Everywhere I looked, there were signs of people engaged in the first steps of recovery—emptying out their homes of items damaged by water.

As I made my way into Little Ferry, I started to see furniture and household items sitting in front yards and on sidewalks. Exercise machines, dining tables, mattresses, carpeting, pictures, bedspreads, and other possessions were stacked on sidewalks waiting to be picked up by a trash truck.

People's water-damaged belongings piled up on the sidewalk, waiting to be picked up.

Every street was lined with personal belongings. It was clear that water damage was the primary issue, and I would soon learn about the devastation it had caused. As I passed a street called Mehrhof, I almost stopped immediately but decided to keep driving. I told myself that if I found this road again, I would turn onto it. Fresh, thick mud seemed to be everywhere as I made my way past the Meadowlands waterway areas.

I passed a public park or ball field filled with cars as far as I could see. New cars, old cars, SUVs—it looked like a used car lot. But where were the people? My first thought was that there was no way that anyone would be playing ball of any kind today. Why would anyone want to leave a car in this park? I made my way around the town and decided that talking with someone else would help get me to the right place.

As I approached Mehrhof for the second time, the street now seemed vaguely familiar. Then I turned left and immediately noticed a man climbing down from the telephone pole nearest to me. I stopped in the street and told him that I wanted to start grilling food for people but needed to know where the worst devastation was. He said, "You are in the worst area inland from the path of the storm. In fact, if you had been here earlier today, you wouldn't be on this street at all. It had several feet of water on it, and our utility company is just now getting in the area to assess the damage.

"However, do you see the utility truck down the left hand side of the street? That guy is my boss. He has a map of the areas nearby and will tell you where to go." That felt like the first sign that I could be near my destination and could soon shut the engine off and get started.

I proceeded to the next truck and stopped in the middle of the street to speak with the utility manager standing near a telephone pole. I said, "Sir, I spoke with your co-worker down the street, and he sent me to ask you where the worst area of devastation is. He said that you have a map of the entire area and that you will send me to the best place for me to get started cooking. I have traveled three days and covered over 1,300 miles to come and cook for people affected by the storm. I have a gas grill and an LP gas tank, and my truck is loaded with pork chops and hot dogs."

The man interrupted me before I was done speaking. Without looking at a map, he said, "You are in the right place. This is where you are supposed to be. Park your vehicle in that parking space and come to the back of my truck. I have something for you." I was a little uncomfortable with his prophetic comment but did as he suggested and parked. I walked around to the back of his truck where I noticed his equipment including wiring, wire stretchers, muddy boots, shovels, and some other hand tools.

He then reached into the bed of the truck and pulled out a huge aluminum pan filled to the top with freshly grilled, honey barbequed chicken wings. The pan weighed about ten pounds and was topped with aluminum foil as though it had just been delivered by a restaurant. It had tape on all four corners to keep the top secure, and it had not even been opened. He handed this incredible gift to me and said, "Here, these are for you."

I was amazed and said, "Are you kidding? This is hot. Unbelievable! Where did this come from?" He smiled and said, "A lady just drove up within the last ten minutes and brought me the chicken for my employees. I told her that the only employee I have is the guy down the street you just spoke with. She insisted that I take it anyway. I now understand that it was meant for you—this is your first food donation. It should give you plenty of time to get your grill set up and start cooking." As soon as he handed me the pan, he got back in his truck and went down the street. I put this generous donation on my tailgate.

I felt a rush of energy and a hope that I might be in the right place as the man had said. The surge of excitement moved me to immediately knock on the doors of two homes on the south side of the street nearest my truck. I waited and waited, but there was no answer at either door.

I was discouraged, so I decided to get back in the truck. I reclined my seat a few inches. I was paralyzed with several emotions at the same time. I was exhausted from only three hours of sleeping in the truck on Friday morning, driving east from

Philadelphia back to the Jersey beaches only to see the same flooded water sights as the night before, heading north up the beaches, making a wrong exit, and going over the Verrazano-Narrows Bridge into Brooklyn and now back to Jersey. So, what was the problem?

I had just met a guy who seemed to be planted directly in my path for some purpose of this trip. Where did he come from? How would he know that I was in the right place? How could he possibly have pulled out this ten-pound container of cooked chicken from the back of a muddy utilities service truck? And why did he speak with me like he had been waiting for me?

I began to experience an adrenaline-like feeling of excitement, uncertainty, and fortune all converging in my mind at the same time. I was overwhelmed and needed to know what to do next. My mind was spinning in turmoil and tumult. I asked myself, "What if this isn't the right place? What if I am mistaken for trying to help? God, it seems like this is your plan, but what if it's not? Should I just set everything up right here along the street? I don't know what to do."

I began to feel a heaviness filling the truck and pressing against my body. This feeling, along with my exhaustion, caused me to be motionless for several minutes. I made a weak attempt to raise my arm to open the door, but it felt numb. I decided to wait just two more minutes. Finally, I heard His voice speaking to my heart as clearly as if He were sitting in the seat next to me say, "I HAVE BEEN WITH YOU EVERY MINUTE. YOU HAVE TRIED TO CALL SEVERAL PEOPLE TO MAKE YOUR TRIP OFFICIAL. I AM NOT LEAVING YOU. SEE THE HOUSE DIRECTLY ACROSS THE STREET? GO KNOCK ON THAT DOOR, AND I WILL SHOW YOU WHAT I AM GOING TO DO." The voice was unbelievable, and yet, distinctly clear in my consciousness.

The sound of His voice reminded me of being at the Indiana State Fair when someone turns on the public address system to make an announcement. You know that the minute the person starts to talk, even if quietly, the sound is going to fill the entire fairground. And while that's the best metaphor I can think of, it is still lacking. The voice had volume but was not loud. It was quiet, powerful, vast, surreal, eerie, and everywhere all at the same time.

I shot straight up in my partially reclined seat to see if I was okay. I catapulted into absolute awe. God had just told me to go across the street, and I believe that when you hear God telling you to do something, it is highly recommended to do as instructed.

Slowly, I moved as directed and approached the house. I was met at the door by a woman who said, "Hi, can I help you with something?" I said, "Yes, ma'am, you might think that I am crazy, but I am from Indiana, and I brought a grill, pork chops, hot dogs, and other food supplies. I am here to start cooking for people in this area."

She was clearly shocked but looked up in the sky, with arms extended upward and outward, and said, "Oh my God!" She embraced me immediately, but briefly, and pointed her finger at me and said, "Stay right there. I am going to get my son and husband. By the way, I am Charlotte."

At this point, I thought I must be at the right place. She soon returned with her husband, Roy, and son Ryan who shook hands with me in the front yard and treated me as though I was a family member who had just returned home. The three of them sprang into action and started going up and down the street encouraging everyone to come out and have something to eat. Within minutes, people started gathering nearby with many of them offering to help in any way they could.

All of a sudden, it seemed like time stood still. My journey had ended, and it was grill on. (I knew that Susan would call, and I would have the answer: "Yes, I found the spot, and I am cooking.")

I got the barbecued chicken wings from the back of my truck and began serving them. Starting with the donated food gave me time to set up the grill. It didn't take long for more people to start showing up. I felt like I was selling food, but it was free for the asking. It was now 4:10 p.m. and the wind had picked up, and the pleasant temperature had turned a little chilly.

The first people to arrive were the neighbors on the corner. "Mayer" and I connected immediately, and he volunteered to cook so that was even better. He loaded the first batch of pork chops on the grill, and the smoke started to roll. I stayed busy every second with greeting people, loading the grill with more meat when Mayer needed me to, and keeping plates from blowing away.

Another group of neighbors from across the street showed up and volunteered to help, and pretty soon we had a canvas cover over the area and battery-powered Chinese lanterns. As people arrived, it was clear that they were more than just interested in what was going on—they wanted to help. The cover provided a break from the wind and gave people a place to stand and talk. Groups of people started to arrive in a steady stream. Three or more at a time arrived, and a line of people wanting food started to grow.

Everyone seemed to be enjoying themselves, laughing and having fun. At times, I heard people talking to each other saying, "Hi, I live across the street, and it's nice to finally make your acquaintance," or "I have seen you at the store a few times." While they lived in the same area, some of the neighbors were meeting each other for the first time.

Others soon learned that I was an easy target to direct humor at, so they started laughing about my sojourn that day that had begun about 6:00 a.m. in Philadelphia and ended in Little Ferry—a trip that normally would take about two hours. I loved it, and I didn't care at all. Their good-natured banter about the guy from

Indiana gave them a little break from the problems they were facing.

THE DAMAGE REPORT

Mehrhof is a fairly wide street, and emergency vehicles were in the area and busy the entire evening. Stories poured in about stress-related problems caused by the storm, from strokes and heart attacks to depression. Nobody was immune to the aftermath. Everyone with a basement had the same problem—flooding. Although the water had subsided, there was standing water four to five feet deep in every basement. Compounding the situation, water pumps were not available, electricity was not on, gas was rationed to first responders, and cell towers were only working part of the time.

I heard a tragic story about a teacher whose husband had died two weeks before the storm leaving her with two teenagers. The two cars they drove had been ruined by the flooding and would be heading to the trash compactor. (The following week, this woman's home burned down.)

The first responders in Bergen County and Little Ferry were busy all evening. The sirens were so loud on the fire trucks that when they drove by, my clothing vibrated from the powerful, high decibel noise, which about deafened me.

A policeman stopped by around 6:00 p.m. He asked me to help keep people off the street because the line for food had gotten really long—and all the emergencies increased the possibility of someone being injured. Charlotte immediately came up behind me and said, "Hey, what did that cop just say?" I thought she was being very protective and wondered if she was going to be my "guardian angel" while I was there. I said, "We are cool, it's all good."

The grill that I bought at Sam's was doing a great job, and with the donated chicken and pork chops, people were crazy about how great the food was. One guy walked up to me and said, "Look at this pork chop." He took a plastic fork and pushed it into the chop to show me how tender it was. He said that he had never had pork chops that tender.

We had plenty of food, but the trash bags were filling up. People kept coming and stayed in line while waiting to get something to eat. As Mayer was cooking, I tried to serve food and hug people and listen to their stories. More people kept coming, and the line made its way around the corner. It had begun to look like a crowd.

I noticed that a utility worker on a pole about 250 feet from where I was standing was in direct line with the smoke when we opened the lid on the grill. I would open the lid, and a huge cloud of smoke would engulf this guy while he was repairing electrical connections. I asked him if he wanted something to eat. He graciously declined until I could talk him into one hot dog. When he finished the repair, he was humble and jovial about the entire matter.

The night went on in laughter and fun. Yes, fun was possible after the storm. Finally, I had a few seconds that I wasn't talking to anyone. Ryan tugged on my arm and said, "Come with me, I want to show you something." We walked a short distance to the center of the street and looked toward New York City. "Have you looked down the street at all tonight?" I had not. I really didn't know where I was in relation to anything else. "What do you see at the end of the road?" I asked, "Is that the Empire State Building?" He said, "It is and I thought you might like to see that."

The beautiful New York City skyline at night is spectacular from any location, but it was especially meaningful to have it in such plain view at the end of the street. The sight and the moment were breathtaking. I had a sense of peace, and in that moment I felt like I was in the right place at the right time.

Around 9:30 p.m., I noticed the line slowing a bit, and we shut the grill off. Someone suggested moving my truck into the driveway, and I did so. Mayer had already left because he had to go to work early Saturday morning, so we picked up several volunteers who helped clean things up.

MEETING THE VOLUNTEERS

A couple, Joe and Lisa, had seen the commotion from down the street. They arrived with their neighbors, Patty and Marty. Joe introduced himself and said, "Hey, I love to cook, and I did a lot of it when I worked for the fire department. I will be glad to help you tomorrow. Also, if you need a hot shower, just come down one block to our home." I had learned to never turn away a volunteer so I said, "Great, I will be up early, so come any time you like." Several of the people asked if I needed a place to sleep, but I was happy just to stay right where I was with Charlotte and Roy along with their sons Ryan, Brett, and Aron—a decision that wouldn't change for the next five days.

We had worked extremely hard for several hours and made quite a mess. We spent another hour with the cleanup and heated water on the grill in order to wash the pans. We needed to get everything ready in case a lot of people showed up the following day.

Lisa was anxious to get home to start baking, which was her specialty. They had a gas oven, so she was able to cook. A few other people remained and sat around in the driveway where we had two firepits with wood that someone had donated. I noticed that it wasn't regular fire wood—it was someone's bamboo floor that had been previously submerged in a water-soaked basement. They had pulled the floor up and left the wood outside for a few days to dry. It was amazing how much heat it generated.

The bamboo flooring popped loudly and shot sparks in the air under the crisp, starlit night. The air was cooled by the water, which was only a few blocks away, and the temperature dropped into the mid-forties.

Our crew was now relaxing and telling stories, laughing and having fun. We were like employees in a restaurant after the crowd went home. We knew by food counts that we had fed over 300 people that evening. Ryan had the most stories because he coached the local football team. Some kids from the team had helped, and they had heard a lot about what people were going through. We were all beginning our new "family time" as though it was a reunion and I was the "relative from Indiana." The time had arrived to put our spatulas down.

I realized that I had had nothing to eat and only a bottle of water to drink. As exhausted as I was, I was so thankful to be in the right place. I knew it in my mind, and more importantly, I knew it in my heart.

The night wore on, and so finally by about 11:00 p.m., everyone was ready to go to bed. I was so tired that I didn't know what planet I was on. I slept on the living room floor in my sleeping bag. Charlotte found an inflatable bed, so I was never really just on the floor. The last thing she said was, "The thermostat shows fifty-two degrees, so can I get you an extra blanket?" I don't remember answering her. It was lights out, curtains. Fire trucks continued roaring down the street all night. I heard one, and that was it.

MIRACLES ON MEHRHOF

Saturday Morning

The next morning, I got up around 6:45 and tried to do something with my hair that now looked a bit like a bird's nest. I was so sore with tension in my neck and tired from too little sleep that I got back in my sleeping bag. I rested until a cute little puppy named Mattie, who looked like Toto from *The Wizard of Oz*, got on my sleeping bag to snuggle with me. This little dog, when excited, could jump vertically two feet off the floor over and over and over. Her piercing bark could hurt your ears. But for now, she was calm and totally content, so I fell asleep. When Charlotte got up, she took Mattie to the door, and they both went outside.

I got up, and the tile floor was like ice to walk on. I shaved with water that was equally as cold. It was very difficult at the least. I climbed back into my jeans and a sweat shirt, which would be the rule for the next few days. No fashion contest or worries about what anyone else thought. I walked out into the driveway to greet the morning—chilly, brisk, and a salt-water smell that I had already become familiar with. I walked to the end of the driveway and looked to my left across the water. In the distance, the Empire State Building stood as a great American icon. I remember that I had visited the building on our senior class trip with several friends from high school.

Someone that Charlotte knew found out about what we were doing and offered the use of a large grill and LP gas tank. Ryan and Brett jumped on the idea, but they needed my truck to pick everything up. So they drove off and returned about thirty minutes later, and cooking was about to go from elementary to advanced. It took all of us to unload the grill because it was enormous! We were all giving each other a high five because we were ready.

I needed coffee. Since we had no gas or electricity, Charlotte and I went to the only donut shop that was open—most restaurants and businesses in the area were so flooded that they couldn't open their doors. We went in and got in line and asked to speak with a manager. Charlotte, thinking ahead, asked for a donation so we would have something for anyone who showed up early. We left with plenty of donuts and coffee to feed the volunteers as we were setting up for the people who were about to converge on us.

When we got back to the house, Joe had already arrived. He had coolers open and was checking out the new grill. Ryan, Aron, and Brett were helping Roy clean out their basement. The electrical box had been completely submerged, so they pulled all connections and let them dry out before attempting to try them again.

Joe helped me unload the supplies I had picked up in Philadelphia including boxes of hamburgers, hot dogs, potato chips—the items that define the American appetite. He wanted everything unloaded, arranged, and organized. Joe was there to do battle with hunger, and he would win.

Joe had already cracked open the gas valve and lit this titanic of a grill that would be put to work for the next twelve hours. I walked in the house for a few minutes for coffee, and when I got back, there was a woman asking Joe what time we were going to start grilling. Although he had started it just to test it, he decided to go ahead and put the first hot dog on. Lisa stayed at their place, so she could make bread. She and Joe were lucky to have gas and a way to bake, and bake, and bake.

9:30 a.m.

The place was getting busy now that the grill was set up and smoke was rolling. Joe was really not setting up to start serving—he was trying to cook ahead. The day was pleasant but with cool winds.

Soon, there were lots of people in the area milling about, something similar to a carnival where many attractions are happening at the same time. We heard that New Jersey Governor Chris Christie was in the area, and we saw camera crews and television trucks going up and down all the streets. Several of the major networks—ABC, NBC, Telemundo—were there.

My phone rang, and it was the mayor of Little Ferry, Mauro Raguseo, who could not have been more kind. He wanted me to know that he would be coming over after he spent time with the governor and other dignitaries. He said that anyone who makes Little Ferry residents friends is automatically his friend. I told him that he would have a hot dog waiting for him. I figured that he was covered up with questions and complaints about the situation and could use a break and friendly conversation.

Almost every home remained with no electricity. Everyone seemed to be busy going somewhere with a lot of interest in the governor's entourage. Most of the residents were hoping to ask questions about state and federal funds that would be available for Little Ferry residents.

Big trucks with car haulers headed to the ball field to pick up more cars and more cars. We learned that when the brackish saltwater hits the electrical systems and engine's "brain," the car can later malfunction even after the saltwater is gone.

Cars at the ball field looked fine but had been ruined by seawater and would be picked up and crushed.

The insurance companies were totaling cars and paying the owners. They were then contracting haulers to go pick up the "dead cars" and take them to be crushed. This prevented anyone else from buying one of these cars with its inherent risks. This tragedy triggered a car rental boon, and there were leased cars all around. A next door neighbor had lost his new Nissan and replaced it with an older Lincoln.

Most homes were damaged too, and there were very sad stories of loss up and down every street. Charlotte and Roy lost two boilers—valued at more than $8,000—that they had used for heating their home. An electrician could have easily charged $3,000 or more for labor to repair the wiring. Thankfully, there were several electricians in the household who would be able to do the work at no cost.

Their house had been the family home for several generations, starting with Charlotte's grandfather. Her family had a long history of involvement in the community. I wondered if it was just a coincidence that I ended up here. Or had God really led me here?

Out in the street, the activity was picking up. The traffic was busy as fire trucks with blaring sirens roared down the street. People who had come out to eat the night before were coming back to eat and visit—maybe because they remembered the pork chops from the night before.

Pauley and Kenny showed up early to offer their assistance. Pauley lived down the street, and he and Kenny had an electrical and heating business. Kenny had driven over fifty miles just to help and hang out with us. The flood water penetrated the area so deeply that their services would be needed more when electricity was restored and people had no standing water in the basements.

I felt a special connection with each volunteer. Something about their desire to help our efforts was a way to pay "love" forward, or return to someone else what had been given to them. I could see a glow within them. All of the volunteers laughed a lot. They were finding joy in serving, and so was I. There was a special bond from working together so that everyone could benefit from our collaborative effort.

We were set up along the edge of the house facing Mehrhof. The driveway was about eighty feet long, which helped break the wind and protect the firepits that we would light later in the day. The entire grill was covered with food as more people arrived to eat. Buns and supplies surrounded the cooks' area.

Joe had created a "cocoon" to work in so that all his supplies were within reach. Plates and forks were nearest the food, and bottles of water and chips and other condiments were on a long table across from where we were cooking.

If Joe took a break from cooking, it was important not to move stuff around because he needed to know where things were. When he cooked, he required organization, and that was fine with me. He reviewed this with me when I took over and moved his chair. He was giving me a dose of "Joisey" attitude that I had fallen in love with the minute I arrived. His ability to be in charge and his enthusiasm were exactly what I needed as I helped young and old with plates, buns, chips, and whatever.

Charlotte and Roy's driveway quickly filled up as people arrived to get something to eat.

Lisa was busy with her "famous breads" that she kept bringing to us fresh from the oven. Cookie and brownie donations also started showing up. So it was kind of like a buffet with all sorts of items.

Things were going great until we noticed our meat supplies. More and more people were lining up, and our meat was running low. First, we finished off the pork chops that I had brought from home. Then, we threw out the empty box that the hot dogs came in, and we were down to our last box of 150 hamburgers that I had bought in Philly.

So what do we do now? Someone needed to make a run for more meat. My truck had gas, which was still a rare item. We heard that there were still long lines of people with five-gallon cans trying to get gasoline. Charlotte came up to me and said, "You are the only one who has gasoline. Could we borrow your truck and go try to find someplace that would possibly give us a food donation?" Without a thought, I handed her the keys and away she and a few others went. My thoughts were now on the line of people that was growing into the next street.

We started to hear from some people in line that Facebook stories were circulating about the relief effort and the grilled meats. The pace of the day was beginning to accelerate—it was exhilarating! When people got something to eat, they also came to shake hands, say "thank you," get hugs, or share the stories of what they were dealing with. The sadness from the storm damage seemed to be temporarily on hold. At times, it felt like listening and giving hugs were more important than the food.

Charlotte and her crew went to Costco (about twenty minutes away) and asked to speak with the manager. When he arrived, Charlotte explained about the vast number of people surrounding the house in line to eat and that she was wondering if we could have a food donation. His reply was, "Ma'am, we have been asked that question all day. It has been hard to do, but I have had to say no and turn people away."

At this point, the angel converted to pit bull and said, "You are not understanding the situation here. The reason we are asking about the donation is that we lost our electricity days ago, and there is a guy sleeping on my floor in a sleeping bag in fifty-two degrees. He has driven all the way from Southern Indiana and brought a grill and meat and was grilling last night and is grilling more today." At this moment, the manager interrupted her and said, "Are you talking about David Gregory?" She was amazed and said, "Yes I am. How do you know him?" He said, "I heard about him from the stories on Facebook. Please bring your truck around, and I will get someone to help us load you up."

He loaded the truck as if he was making sure we wouldn't need anything else. He started with a huge Rubbermaid deck storage unit for the supplies and filled it with 750 hot dogs, along with buns and condiments to go with them, and cases and cases of water. It was a massive amount of food that would keep us feeding others for the next couple of days.

The cooking crew included (from left to right) Ryan, Joe, Pauley, me, Aron, and Kenny.

When I saw the truck coming down the street, I couldn't believe it. Joe was amazed, too. All of the volunteers worked to get the truck unloaded knowing that the line was long and getting longer. More people kept coming, and we had two people cooking at all times. I wanted to meet as many people as possible, so I was encouraged to reposition myself at the sidewalk next to the street.

The mayor, who reminded me of a younger version of Al Pacino, stopped by to greet everyone. He is the youngest mayor in the history of Little Ferry and has a huge heart for the community. During the storm surge and the rising water in their own home, his wife had to swim to the neighbor's house just to be with someone. The mayor had stayed busy that night just trying to check on many of the people hardest hit from the disaster within the 1.25 square miles of Little Ferry. It was easy to see why this man is loved by so many.

Charlotte, Little Ferry Mayor Raguseo, and me.
Joe is working the grill.

As I stood there, a guy walked up and introduced himself as being with the *New York Daily News*. (I had no idea who he was or that they are one of the largest newspapers in the country.) He was a classmate of Ryan's, and he wanted to do a story on us and produce a video as well as a news article that would appear online.

Without thinking, I consented and stood alone in the corner of our now highly populated driveway while his interview took place. He recorded it on his iPad that he held just a few inches from my face—which was nerve-racking at the very least. I didn't have the luxury of thinking about what was going on or preparing my responses. I was more concerned about how Joe was doing with the grilling of the food and nothing else. In fact, I kept speaking to Joe during the interview, and I was reminded to finish the interview as quickly as possible, and then I could get back to cooking.

THE SPANISH PRAYER

A short time later, one of the volunteers came to me and said, "A Spanish woman and her daughter are in line, and they need to speak with you as soon as possible. The older lady is in poor health. She has brought you a prayer, so it is important for you to go to her as quickly as you can. Oh, there is one more thing . . . she doesn't speak a word of English." I was led to where the two women were anxiously waiting. The daughter was taller and maybe in her mid-forties while her mother could have been in her mid-sixties. The daughter introduced them speaking in broken English and said, "My mother has doctors' orders to stay in bed. She is not well and takes several prescription drugs.

"She read about you from Facebook stories, and she was so moved that she told me that she must come to you because she had been inspired with a prayer, just for you. I helped her get ready, and getting here has been a challenge. She does not speak a word of English. Do you speak Spanish?" I said, "No." The daughter then asked if I could get an interpreter so that I could understand.

Without hesitation, the older lady reached up as I leaned over, and she gave me a big hug, nearly pulling me over since she was much shorter. She immediately started her prayer by speaking in Spanish, but I had to stop her. I told her daughter to please wait just a minute until an interpreter could get in place to give me the English version. I turned around, and Ryan was right behind me. I grabbed him and asked him to get me someone to translate the Spanish. He had several football players who were bilingual, and one volunteered at Ryan's request, so he brought a tall football player back to the Spanish lady.

She grabbed me again and pulled me back down toward her. She was on my left at about four foot eleven, and he was on my right at about six foot five. He leaned in to hear her start praying with her soft, delicate voice. He began to interpret what he heard as she continued into her prayer. It was as if I was inside a stereo with Spanish in one ear and English in the other ear. At a point, however, it sounded like the young man began his own prayer. I closed my eyes and heard a symphony of the most beautifully orchestrated music of words that I have ever heard.

Suddenly, I found myself in a center of peace and love. In this space, I was filled with a great sense of calm. The prayer concluded, and I hugged and thanked the woman and the young man and went back to the cooking area to check on Joe. The woman and her daughter turned and headed home, walking slowly.

I returned to the driveway and started stacking clothing that someone had dropped off on the tables where the food supplies were. People were now donating clothing and other items just to be helpful. A policeman stopped out front, got out of his car, and said, "Hey, I have heard about you. A woman just gave me four sandwiches in this sack. I have only eaten one of them, but they are delicious. Please accept this donation and give these three to someone else who needs this more than me."

This simple act of kindness touched me so deeply that I got choked up. I couldn't audibly say "thank you" but hugged him and tried anyway. My emotions were becoming more prevalent as the day wore on and more unusual events were happening. I needed to stay focused so I could be emotionally supportive to the people who were sharing stories of loss and devastation from the storm.

About that time, I saw three young women coming from the east side of the street with grins from ear to ear. They were walking as quickly as possible as though they were competing in a speed-walking contest. I had no idea they were actually walking toward me. One of them pointed her finger at me and giggled at the same time. They were still about twenty feet away, and one of the girls excitedly said, "You are the guy. You're the guy we are looking for. You are David, aren't you?" I answered, "Yes, I am. What are you girls up to? Did you get lost?" She confidently said, "Oh no, we are not lost at all. We drove sixty-five miles just to say hello and bring you a food donation. This story has circulated four times on each of our Facebook pages. We are sure that this story has been circulated thousands of times."

I was smiling, and likely beaming, at this point so I asked, "What makes you think that?" Her answer was, "Well, I only have 3,000 friends on Facebook, but my sister (pointing to the next girl) has 4,700 friends, and my cousin (pointing to the third girl) has over 5,000 friends on Facebook! So if the story circulated four times on each of our pages, your story has been circulated thousands of times.

"We thought we could help you, so here is what we did. We got up early and worked all day to make one hundred peanut-butter-and-jelly sandwiches. We wrapped each one in its own sealed bag, and each bag was put in a sack. This is a donation for anyone who might not like grilled food." The sentiment was overwhelming, and each of them gave me a big hug.

They carefully placed each sandwich in a stacked, concise order, making them easy to hand out. As soon as they were done, they disappeared into the busy landscape of activities of the day, and I didn't see them again.

The peanut-butter-and-jelly-sandwich girls.

I quickly moved on to chat with another group of people. One of the volunteers came up behind me and asked, "When is the last time you had something to eat?" That was something that I had not thought about. She took me by the arm and said, "Sit down and please eat." She stuck a bottle of water in one hand and a hot dog in the other. It would be the only food that I would eat that day. It was unusual for me not to be hungry, but the idea of eating was as foreign as the thought of going home.

So with a little nourishment, I returned to the line. Firemen started showing up, and it was great to see them taking a break. These guys would jump into a burning building to save a life and absolutely think nothing about it. Most of them knew Joe from when he worked at the firehouse in nearby Ridgefield.

What the first responders saw and dealt with after the storm was almost impossible to talk about. Stories were starting to circulate about people knocking on the doors of residents and entering their homes. The people doing this had FEMA (Federal Emergency Management Agency) badges, but they were not from FEMA. They then robbed residents of whatever they had left.

A retired fireman who drove fifty miles to visit was laughing about my Purdue sweatshirt. He said, "I read about your story and knew you were from Indiana. So I thought my Indiana University hat would look good with your Purdue sweatshirt since they are big-time rivals, and I really want a picture to send my son." I said, "That is great because I'll send a copy to my son. He graduated from IU, and my daughter graduated from Purdue."

It occurred to me that I had not heard the sound of any music all day since nobody had electricity. My remedy to that was that I wanted to hear Mark Knopfler (Dire Straits), whose music was on my iPod in the truck. I turned on the music, and sounds from the album *On Every Street* wafted through the air.

I looked up, and a man with sky blue eyes approached me in the front yard. He had tears streaming down his face. He said, "I absolutely love Dire Straits and Mark Knopfler. Your music took me back to another day." I told him, "You are preaching to the choir." He asked if he could just "hang out" for a while. I said, "I am staying several more days, so you can stay the entire time if you like. I'm happy surrounded by food, friends, and conversation." I tried to fix him a plate of food, but he didn't want anything to eat. He just wanted to talk.

After about thirty minutes, he looked at me again, and I could tell that he wanted to say something very personal. Tears started streaming down his face again. He said, "I just buried my dad on Tuesday, and it was extremely hard on us. My mom is now in intensive care at the hospital. She is at the point of death, and other family members are with her.

"I have felt so isolated because we lost our cars in the flooding saltwater, and we have been dealing with so much emotion. We have no idea what is going to happen, but we are hoping that my mom will wait on us to get to the hospital. The thought of her passing without me saying goodbye is too much to consider."

All of a sudden, like an alarm just rang, I looked at him and felt a surge of emotion— as though we were the only people there and we were somehow in a different space. I looked at him and asked, "Are you here by yourself?"

He looked surprised but said, "My wife is here with me." I said, "Please get her right now. I need you both, and we are going to pray about this—right now." My response surprised me too. I have never said anything like that before. One of the volunteers heard me say this but quietly watched and started to pray. (I learned that later.)

He quickly returned with his wife and introduced her. I felt an urgency to pray that I did not understand. I said, "Guys, we are going to act like we're on a football field and get in a huddle." I heard his wife say, "Uh, okay." So, the three of us huddled up, and I started praying. I can't tell you what I said in that prayer, but I can tell you what I heard my voice say to them after the prayer was over.

I got in his face and firmly clutched his shoulder with my hand. Blue eyes to blue eyes, I heard my voice say the following: "YOU DO NOT HAVE TO WORRY ABOUT GETTING TO VISIT WITH YOUR MOTHER. SHE IS GOING TO WAIT ON YOU, AND YOU WILL GET INTO THE HOSPITAL AND JOIN YOUR FAMILY, AND YOU WILL HAVE YOUR VISIT WITH YOUR MOTHER. AFTER YOU VISIT FOR A SHORT WHILE, SHE WILL BE LEAVING."

This event happened so fast that I was stunned to hear what I had just heard. It was my voice but not my thoughts. How could that have possibly just happened? Why did I say that? It was as though we were in another realm, and in that space, and in that moment that I shared with these two loving people, it seemed that nothing else existed.

They left immediately, and who could blame them? They were coming over just to say hello, and I seemed to have changed what was a pleasant visit into a mission of expediency. I quickly dismissed what had just happened or, more importantly, the "impact" of what had just happened.

I moved on because a fire truck pulled up in front of the house and stopped for a minute. A mountain of a man with a heart of the purest gold opened the door of that truck and got out. He wore the kind of bibs that are worn for fighting fires. He had removed his coat, and his bibs were flopping downward on his stomach. He was still wearing his boots.

He said "I have heard about what's going on here, and I'm not here to eat your food. I am here to hug the man who cared so much about us that he came to help." He embraced me with a "bone crushing" hug, and he held me for a while and then told me that he loved me. With tears rolling out of my eyes, I tried to say, "Thank you," and "I love you." He said that he would be back with his brother later that evening. When they both showed up, we fixed a plate of food for each of them. They sat down and relaxed by the fire with us.

Another visitor was a schoolteacher, and she was from a nearby town, maybe fifteen minutes away. She had brought donations with her and returned the next day with more items. She had three young children, and the bonus: they were triplets. The kids were so sweet, and the little boy ran up to me and gave me a hug.

It was now fun when I started to recognize my new friends. Maybe I didn't remember each one's name, but a special connection was made with each person we encountered.

Another fireman came by with his wife and two children. Their daughter had a cute hat in the shape of a kitten. The little girl was having fun. She would take her hat and throw it up in the air, and it would hit the ground. Then, she would go over to her mom and giggle. I picked her hat up off the ground and brushed it off. I tried to caution her that her mom might not like it if her new pink hat got dirty, but she didn't care. I would give it back to her, and once again, she would throw it back up in the air. Acting silly and making her and others laugh provided such a great escape from the heavy situations that I had seen and heard about that day.

The crowd and the food prep were great, but the effort had put tension in my neck and shoulders. In fact, at one point my neck was so stiff that it looked like I was suffering from an accident or partial paralysis. A chiropractor was in line for a hot dog and noticed my head leaning to the left. He said, "Step over here, and let me work on that neck." I did so eagerly. Within a few minutes, I was able to move freely. Somehow, my energy level was good, and my stamina seemed to hit high gear as daylight was turning to darkness. Still, a yard and a driveway full of people remained enjoying the company of one another.

A wheelbarrow became a makeshift cooler as supplies grew.

We watched our food count, but Joe knew that with the 750 hot dogs that had been donated earlier that day, we were good. I asked Joe how many people we had fed. By 6:00 p.m., we had served 800 with maybe 100 still in line. The line of people was growing because of dinner. Joe and his crew had done nothing but serve. They started kidding me about my mannerisms and Hoosier accent. Ryan was leading the effort at imitating me, adding to the lightheartedness.

We had found a few minutes to get to know each other. I respected the fact that Ryan was so interested in the lives of the teenagers he coached—knowing the importance to them of grades and their family lives as well. "Coach Ike," as the kids called him, was there for them, and they knew it. He encouraged training and physical development, but I appreciated that he placed even more value on moral and character development. I was very impressed with his maturity, leadership, and love of serving others.

I made my way back to the front of the driveway to help serve the group of people winding down the street again. Joe and his assistants had cooked ahead, and we were easily ready for 200 more people. I was busy meeting more people when all of a sudden, I looked out of the corner of my left eye. Here came my blue-eyed friend and his wife rapidly making their way toward me, and in an instant, my entire memory was restored from what had happened earlier in the day—when I prayed for this man, his wife, and the situation with his mother.

I absolutely panicked as I replayed the scenario in my mind. If there had been a hole in the ground, I would have jumped in it. How could I have said the things I said? After all, it did come out of my mouth. When he got to me, I could see tears, but also his smile was beaming like "Sonshine."

He immediately grabbed me and hugged me intensely. He said, "Thank you so much for what you said. It happened exactly the way you said it would. We were able to get into the hospital and join our family. Mom had waited, and I was able to visit with her, and after a short while, she left just as you said. We hated to see her go, but I was so happy that she waited and we could say goodbye."

I said, "I am amazed that everything happened the way you described, but you need to know one thing—I did not say that." We both knew that the words came out of my mouth, but we also knew that I was incapable of knowing. He and his wife hugged me again and told me that they loved me, and suddenly, they seemed to disappear as quickly as they had returned.

I had to sit down and take a break. I just needed to stop and breathe and took a break of about ten minutes. Then a woman came over to meet me, introduced herself, and asked, "Would it be okay if I stay around for a while? I would just like to ask you some questions about yourself and your family. Is that okay?" My standard answer was, "I will be here all night." She said, "My husband works until 10:00 p.m. and our kids are busy with school projects, so I have a while to visit."

I pulled a lounge chair from the side of the driveway, and we sat down and began to talk. She seemed comfortable and proceeded to tell me about herself and her family: where they worked, where they had lived, and activities that they enjoyed. She asked the normal stuff that others also wanted to know. Where are you from? Are you married? Do you have kids? What made you come up here? What made you stop in Little Ferry?

I answered all her questions and had her giggling occasionally. But it was apparent that something was bothering her. Her face would beam with smiles and laughter, and yet, her expression seemed to fade away as if there was an underlying pain. I was casual about the conversation, being careful not to question anything personal that she might be feeling.

She continued to share her story, and through her expression, she was visibly beginning to show signs of grieving with tears streaming down her cheeks as she tried to smile. Suddenly, I started to sense the pain that I saw in her. She kept talking, but somehow I was growing more uncomfortable, so I got up out of my chair and stood near it. My perception of her pain changed to discernment of pain and loss. She stood up and continued talking more softly, her voice shaking. The moment of her explaining her sadness had arrived, and although I wanted to avoid hearing it, I sensed the importance of listening and not backing away.

I reached out to hug her and when I did, I felt her distress as she whispered the words that had been too painful to speak out loud, "My best friend was caught up in the surge of the storm on the coast, and two members of her family perished in the incident but she made it. This has just torn my life apart."

After revealing this, she seemed to perk up. She looked refreshed and had a beautiful smile again. She thanked me for visiting with her and turned away to go home. When she let go of me, I almost fell.

Lisa was behind me and grabbed me to keep me from falling. She took my arm and said, "Come with me. We need to go for a walk." I needed a place to collapse, and soon I was walking through Lisa's door where that could happen. The intensity of the stories and the number of people experiencing the destruction of the storm were difficult to take in. I found a place to lie down.

As I lay there, the intensity of the pain of the stories I had heard was overwhelming. Lisa worked in the kitchen on breads and baked goods and then came in to try to console me. I sobbed uncontrollably for five to ten minutes. Lisa said very little, but I was getting a break that I needed. The entire day and all of the stories had culminated in my mind and saturated my whole being.

I remembered listening to Pastor Jeff and Julie when they warned me of turbulent times ahead and that I may call them at any time. This was the time that I felt the need to call. Jeff answered immediately. I was crying (feeling crazy) and relating to him the extent of the suffering and its effect on those of us who were listeners as well. He said that I was there as "hope" to those looking for a shoulder to cry on or an ear to listen. Inside his response, I could hear a smile of approval. After listening for a few minutes, I asked Lisa to speak with Jeff as I tried to collect myself.

When I got back on the phone, Jeff said (in this enormous voice of reason), "I am concerned about your need to be spiritually fed. You don't seem to be grounded." His voice had almost changed in meter and time. He asked if I had a Bible handy, and I said that my phone had an app with the Bible in it. He reviewed some chapters that he thought were best to help me. He explained, "Probably the Old Testament is the best place for some great guidance. I think the best place to start might be the book of Psalms."

He said, "Why don't you start with Psalm 1:1 and just keep reading through it until you are tired, and then get some rest." I agreed but decided to head back to Charlotte's house because I felt like people were in line and I wanted to be there to greet them.

We left Lisa's home and got back to work. At this point, the winds were quite chilly from the water but the fires were burning in the firepits. The bamboo flooring supply was running low, and now people were donating firewood and lumber that had dried out.

Everyone was positioned between houses, out of the wind, and now the evening was winding down. Our helpers were finally getting a well-deserved rest, and yes, even Charlotte was sitting down. I was resting but feeling significant pain in my shoulder and neck area. This did not go unnoticed, and someone began rubbing my neck to help. I started fading into a goo.

As we sat and talked, everything started to become funny. If you stood up and said the word "shoehorn," the entire group would go into hysterical laughter. Some of the comedians in the group stood up and tried to be funny, and they were.

We had enough hot dogs and other food on hand for tomorrow and Monday if needed. We shared stories for an hour or so, and we were later joined by the mayor who wanted to check on us. We fixed more hot dogs immediately for any other latecomers.

We were all amazed about the food replenishment from Costco and the sheer volume of people who had lovingly converged and shared our space. We planned on starting the grill later tomorrow, closer to noon. Some of the houses along the street were starting to show lights inside—meaning that electricity had been restored in a few areas. What that meant for us was that people could prepare their own food and the need for our grill would become less and less.

Around 11:00 p.m., Charlotte stood up and said that everyone needed to go home and get some rest. We all went inside to go to bed. There were emergencies throughout the night, and when the responding vehicles went by, the noise was incredible. The roaring sirens were loud, and the weight of the trucks shook the street. You could feel the vibration, but none of it bothered me. I hit the sleeping bag and conked out.

Sunday Morning

Early the next morning, I felt a familiar little lick, but this time it was on my eyelid. Mattie knew the inside of my sleeping bag was warmer than the house, and she wanted to snuggle. I complied. I got up after daylight and went out to walk and get some exercise.

I turned east and headed toward the direction of the Empire State Building. As I passed the park, a Korean man walked up to me and in very broken English asked, "Are you with the power company?" I said, "No, but I have some experience with wiring." He then asked, "Could you come over to my house and take a look at something?" He shook my hand and said, "My name is Brian."

I made my way up his steps to his door. He looked at me and asked, "Could you please remove your shoes?" It had been a long time since I heard that but gladly agreed. I walked in and introduced myself to his wife, and he asked her to fix us a cup of tea. (Natural gas was working, so she was able to heat water.)

The electrical service had been restored, but then it went back off. I knew very little about why the power was off but showed Brian where the electrical service came in from the utility pole and suggested that the problem was after it got into the house. We inspected two rooms to find the electrical box entrance. I was only making suggestions because I didn't have continuity testers or any other electrical tools.

I asked to use the bathroom and noticed that there was a hair dryer lying on a shelf. Without thinking, and looking at this straw patch on top of my head called hair, I cracked opened the door and said, "Brian, may I wash my hair in your sink and then use your wife's hair dryer?" There was this long pause of silence. He started giggling so loudly, and then he broke out in his native tongue and told his wife something. Then she started laughing so loudly that I started wondering why that question was so funny? He then walked up to the door and said, "We don't have electricity, remember?" Ha ha! I walked out of the restroom and felt like a goofball and probably looked like one.

Brian was laughing so hard that there were tears streaming down his cheeks. His wife could not speak a word of English, but I noticed her trying to contain herself, and out of respect, she turned away and did not face me. I didn't mind at all. Communication would remain a struggle, but I enjoyed a brief visit in the living room with tea. Brian and his wife were originally from the area around Seoul. They had children who were grown, and Brian worked at a shoe store at a nearby mall.

The time came for me to leave. I was convinced that I had not helped them at all, but at least they had a good laugh. I was so numb from sensory stimulation overload that nothing really seemed to matter, but I thought of the saying that "laughter is good for the soul" (and for the Seoulians). I invited them to come down later that day and told them we would be grilling and had plenty of food.

The water department had made several trips down the street in their trucks, and now they honked their horns and waved as they drove by. That was a good feeling, but the stark reality was that Indiana would be in my near future and that was because life was trying to return to a more "normal" mode here in New Jersey. This incredible journey was about to conclude.

When I got back to Charlotte's house, Mattie went nuts and started yelping to go outside. Charlotte came down in a short while to say good morning and take Mattie out. There were two other dogs in the family, so it was a complex people/dog affair just to go outside. Charlotte came back in and sat down in the living room. She just wanted to talk since all of our time had been shared with other people.

She said, "I didn't even do a background check on you, yet you end up on my living room floor." I told her that anyone who is crazy enough to choose to sleep on the floor, no electricity, and fifty-two degrees, needs a psych evaluation, not a background check." We both laughed. This was our time to talk and really learn more about each other.

As we sat there, Charlotte decided to talk about the history of her home. We talked for a short time until I remembered that I had been invited to go to church with Joe and Lisa. They attended the Tenafly United Methodist Church, which was about twenty minutes away. I was hoping to meet the United Methodist Council on Relief (UMCOR) representative from their local church. I had received a lot of calls from people at home who were interested in coming up to help, so I wanted to be able to provide a contact name.

The church was quaint with a diverse group of people who were very friendly. I was greeted by Pastor Beth who said, "Isn't attending another United Methodist Church like coming home?" I agreed that it was. Feeling right at home, I was drafted to sing with the choir, so I didn't really have much time to chat. I needed to practice and get familiar with the music. The choir was great, and with about thirty people, they had a powerful sound. Pastor Beth introduced me as the "guy from Indiana with a grill and a truck."

What she said was clearly in love, kindness, and appreciation for what had happened on Mehrhof and what was happening in the world of volunteerism in New Jersey and New York. Her family had been personally affected by the storm and experienced loss. I was asked to make a few comments about why I was there and what we were doing. I don't remember too many details about what I said but do remember saying that helping someone else will multiply the ways you are helped.

Pastor Beth concluded the service with comments about the effects of the storm, helping others, and the need for all kinds of people with all kinds of talents that everyone can benefit from.

The next part of the morning was the "social hour," which featured food and fellowship. Of course, my plate was not empty, and it was fun to visit. I was fortunate to meet a nice young man who believed his call was to work with youth in the church. He explained to me how he had heard that call and experienced several struggles of his own.

I tried to express how special this type of work is because you are dealing with kids at an impressionable age. Working in the life of a child is sacred. I tried to remember the famous quote from Forest Witcraft but messed some of it up: "A hundred years from now it will not matter what my bank account was, the sort of house I lived in, or the kind of car I drove. But the world may be different because I was important in the life of a child."

After eating and visiting for a while, we made our way back to Mehrhof. It was getting later, and it was about eleven o'clock by the time we got back. I felt certain that the activity in the driveway would be picking up momentum.

When Joe, Lisa, and I arrived, it was obvious that we had missed some action. The first thing that Ryan said to me was that Telemundo wanted an interview with us, and they were planning to come back after I returned from the service. I said that was fine because I was not going anywhere, not moving out of this driveway, not shutting the grill off until we had nobody left to feed.

The day was pleasant and sunny, and the media were swarming. The governor and other dignitaries were visiting the area, and they were not far away. Joe quickly cracked open the gas on the big grill and smoke started to roll. People and service trucks were all over the place as they worked to restore power. Trucks with long platforms designed to haul cars were going up and down the street. Electricians were in the area to see if anyone needed help. Representatives from car rental companies were combing the streets offering discounts for everyone in this area.

In Charlotte's home, the water in the basement had dropped enough to allow access to the electrical box so that the breakers could all be pulled out to dry. Roy, Ryan, and Brett were careful to label each breaker, and they made a nice drainage system inside a Rubbermaid kitchen container. The process was very meticulous and gave me a good feeling about the electricians in the house.

The heating system was a steam and hot water closed loop system, but it had been totally submersed in the brackish-saltwater that flooded the entire area. There would be no resurrection for this system. It would all have to be drained and the boilers replaced. So the guys stayed busy in the basement, and Charlotte and I went outside to get to work.

Charlotte was constantly in need of heated water from one of the three grills we had going. She was using the water to wash the pans and serving utensils, and cold water would not cut the grease at all. We heated the water, and then we could wash quite a bit.

Many people came back to see us from previous visits while others showed up for the first time. Saturday had been filled with stories of loss, but now we started to see signs of hope. A neighbor from a couple of blocks away came by to say, "There are people in my neighborhood saying that they love each other. We don't do that in Jersey." I said, "You do now."

Kenny and Pauley arrived and offered to help in any way. Joe was nicely seated on his "perch." He was ready for business and for people to come through the line. Lisa showed up later to bring more bread, cupcakes, and cobblers. Several other women were organizing the garment table of clothing that had been donated.

Any time that I have been involved in a project requiring so many hours or so much work, someone usually complains (sometimes me). Maybe the complaint is about how someone is feeling, the conditions we are working under, bad weather, extremely cold temperatures, or too much work. This team had no complaints. None. We enjoyed serving others, and it was obvious that the saying, "It is more blessed to give than to receive," was true. The "energy" that gave us strength to persevere also gave us joy.

The firefighters were busy, but sometimes their wives and kids could stop by and have a bite to eat. It seemed like all of the kids liked hot dogs. I had really connected with some of the firefighters with their open displays of affection and pictures and stories of their families. It made me think more about the danger that they deal with every day and whether or not they would be coming home that night.

Their families must live with this uncertainty every day. For them, it goes without saying but it doesn't go without feeling. The daily separation in the marriage is a reminder that anything can happen. Their lives are an example of serving others on an exponential basis. It is the ultimate in giving as all of the first responders risk their own lives, trying to serve and save others. It is also important to remember the dedication of volunteer firefighters and their level of commitment.

The mayor stopped by again for a visit after the governor's entourage left to go to another town. The mayor was extremely busy with a ringing cell phone and his own housing damage. He had to deal with homeowner's issues just like everyone else. He had agencies to contact, forms to fill out, and questions to answer—but he wanted to see how we were doing.

The day continued to be steady but not with the massive amount of people we saw on Saturday. Families were continuing to come by to eat or at least take something home. Our supplies were holding up nicely.

Later in the afternoon, Pastor Beth from church paid us a visit. She brought her camera and stayed busy for more than an hour. She took pictures and spoke with several people about what they were doing and told them how their help with cooking and serving was a blessing to others. She was fun to be around and brought excitement with her. She was wise and offered comfort and sound advice when responding to questions from those who had been affected by the storm. She carefully probed her listeners for signs of depression.

At times, she seemed like the media, interviewing and speaking with young and old, taking pictures and finding something nice to say no matter what. She was not exempt from heartache because so many in her congregation and other people she knew had been affected by the storm—including her own family. I had no idea that what she was really doing was gathering information for her sermon the following Sunday.

The sun was out, but the winds were brisk that day. It was the type of early November day that leads you to wear a coat or sweatshirt. The wind blew our paper plates and napkins around, but it was fairly calm between the houses. The grill billowed smoke, and everyone who visited would come and sit in the driveway near the firepits to keep out of the wind. Joe kept meticulous count on buns and knew that we had served over 300 people although that was a fraction of the 1,000 the day before, but we needed to slow down the pace of the cooking. He returned to his seat from which he would not move unless he needed a break.

Some of the "regulars" started asking "When are you going home?" My standard answer was: "I don't know yet." At this point, I barely remembered having a home, who I was, or where I was from. I was basking in happiness, laughter, fun, and purpose all at once. I loved being there, and leaving was the last thing on my mind.

Leaving meant saying goodbye to all who had just changed my life. I had no idea how hard that was going to be, and I really didn't want to think about it. About that time, Susan called and asked if I knew when I might be coming home. I said, "Not today, and probably not tomorrow, but sometime for sure." (I snickered, and she did not.)

She had said enough that I knew the discussions about my return would increase during subsequent calls. Her questions were founded in love as she knew about everything that had happened and that it all seemed to be part of a bigger plan.

Almost the minute that we said goodbye, my phone rang again and this time it was Bruce from home. He said, "I love what you did by going up there. I saw the story on the news, but I have also seen your heart." I told him "We've been on this path together. Helping after Katrina turned me around, and this is all your fault!"

We both had a good laugh. He said, "You know that I am dying to come up there. I told you no once, and I won't say no again. Please find me a person in the United Methodist system who has a position with UMCOR, and I will contact the person directly and stay in touch with you. Remember, I want to wallow in mud. I want the nastiest 'muck crew' that I can find."

Bruce would crawl in mud to help someone else—he has, does, and will—until he can't crawl any more. (He drove alone to the Dakotas one time to help after a disaster and didn't tell anybody at church. Nobody knew where he was, and he told his wife not to tell anyone.)

This same guy called me after Hurricane Katrina and said, "Please don't say no until I finish my question." I kept quiet. "Why can't we take a double axel trailer and build four shower units, including two for women and two for men, on it and send it to Gulfport, Mississippi, to Trinity United Methodist Church? They are being bombarded with people from all over the world wanting to volunteer, and they have room for them to sleep, but they have no showers."

We talked through the idea and decided to give it a shot. We invited people from church to help, and for several weeks, Bruce's backyard and barn were converted into a construction zone. He was in charge of the building part of the project and his wife, Anne, made sure none of the workers went hungry or thirsty.

One of the Old North United Methodist Church shower trailer work crews, including Bruce (standing in trailer), and his wife, Anne.

The project turned our church into a family. The women got crazy with the ladies' showers down to the color of the corded ropes that held the shower curtains back from the liner. The men didn't seem to be as picky.

A completed shower trailer on location at Trinity United Methodist Church in Gulfport, Mississippi, after Hurricane Katrina.

"Let's talk on your way home, and if you can talk Susan into it, maybe we can plan to return together. But I need a contact with UMCOR." I heard Bruce smiling, and I was so excited by the call. Now, someone is coming back up to this area, and I might be able to come with him. (I would not suggest this the next time Susan called.)

By now, evening was setting in, and the wind stayed strong. Pastor Beth had completed her visit and went home. Several firefighters showed up with their families to see us and spend some time together. Some policemen and one policewoman named Sandy arrived. Poor lady. She got hassled because of her name being like that of the storm.

It was great to see all of the families hanging out together. I acted silly with kids, and they laughed and acted silly with me. So the fathers got in line, and moms and the kids made their way to warm up by the fires. The guys all knew me by now, and I was beginning to learn all of their names, but the word "brother" seemed to cover it.

RIDING WITH ANGELS BEHIND THE SIREN

One of my friends from the fire department was Frank, and he was about the last person in line. He made his way forward with a plate, potato chips, and a hot dog bun open and ready to go. I said, "Please allow me to serve you." I put the hot dog on his bun, and in one second his radio blasted a sound that indicated a "fire run."

I stood still and looked at him, and he said, "Okay mister grillmaster, are you going on a run with me?" Without thinking I said, "Absolutely!" He put down the plate, looked at me and said, "Then start running!" We took off running and turned left on Mehrhoff and headed in the direction of the Empire State Building.

As we passed the first block, a streetlight was illuminating the street (only a handful of lights were on), and I could see that Frank was smiling and could run for another hour as he wasn't even breathing hard. He was tall with an athletic build, so I was hoping that his truck wasn't far away and that I had the breath to get there. As I was huffing and puffing, I said, "Just how many miles away are you parked?" He laughed and said, "Not far."

When we got to his truck, we hopped in and he got on the radio to say, "Headed to the firehouse with the lights flashing and the hammer down." We were only about five minutes from the station. He parked his truck, and we ran inside the Marshal Avenue Firehouse.

With high ceiling and an old antique fire engine, the firehouse—the place from which so many lives have been saved—was an incredible sight. The experience was exciting, and I tried to stay out of the way.

The antique fire truck at Little Ferry Hose Company No. 1.

What I saw next were incredible moments of human precision. Every person was grabbing gear, safety helmets, and passing each other as though it were a choreographed dance. About fifteen to twenty guys were weaving and passing each other at a high rate of speed—and with gear in hand, winding around and not bumping into each other. Two engines would make this run.

I was rushing to keep up with Frank as we headed toward the engine. I took a huge step off the ground and pulled myself up and into the back door of engine number 306. I sat in the middle of three seats facing the rear of the engine. The area was so large that several others could stand or sit. There were three guys in the front seats facing forward and other firemen on the outside rear of the truck.

The driver was reviewing the nature of the run with Frank and the other guys. The detail of the conversation could not have been more refined. Our driver relayed information to Frank, and then a person's name would come up as to what special role he would play on the run. During the middle of the conversation, the fireman in the front passenger seat turned around to me and said, "How are you doing back there? Is everything okay? Above your head is a control for heat if you are cold. The temperature is on the left, and the fan switch is on the right."

I was shocked that anyone recognized that I was even in the truck at all, much less to ask if I was comfortable. I said, "Yes, I am extremely happy. Please don't worry about me. I am fine." I must have looked like a child on a thrilling ride, but I could not stop smiling as my appreciation for first responders was growing by the minute. As I sat there, I kept thinking of these incredible people dedicated to the safety and survival of someone else.

The 70,000 pound engine seemed to rock gently on its air-supported suspension system. The noise must have approached one hundred decibels. With sirens blaring, engines roaring, and horns blowing, we soon arrived at the home.

The nature of the emergency was about a man who had left his generator running in his basement all day. His entire house was filled with carbon monoxide. Nobody knew what we would find once we got to the site.

As soon as we stopped, this precision team went to work. Equipment was unloaded and organized in an expedient manner and placed for easy access for the group that would enter the home. I stayed close to Frank, and he escorted me to the side of the engine that faced the home with the problem. He immediately strapped on a Scott Air Pack, and I assisted him in any way I could.

As he pulled his facemask over his head, he said, "Stay right here and don't get any closer to the house. I will be back." I found a huge running board on the truck to sit on. The lights above my head were as bright as stadium lights illuminating the entire home that they were about to enter. The wind was brisk and blowing steadily, but I was numb with excitement and holding onto every second. The tension peaked as Frank's team got into position to assist him and one other fireman to enter the home. I had the best seat to watch as everything happened.

Members of the Little Ferry Fire Department prepare
to enter a house filled with carbon monoxide.

Frank had a carbon monoxide alarm, similar to a walkie-talkie, on his belt. That alarm was programed to go off upon detecting fifty parts per million (ppm) of carbon monoxide. As the others behind him carefully walked up a steep flight of steps to enter the home, I couldn't help but remember the images of the first responders on 9/11 and how they raced straight up stairways not knowing if they would go home that night.

My heart sank, and I wished that I could have been doing more. Before Frank even touched the handle of the door, his alarm started beeping at a loud volume. That meant that there was enough carbon monoxide inside the house to activate his alarm at fifty ppm outside the house. He quickly turned around to his co-workers and said, "Let's get this place open."

As they made their way inside, the readings went from fifty to 500 ppm! This was clearly enough to kill someone. From their years of experience, they all agreed that the homeowner would not have survived much longer if they had not arrived. Staying in precision, Frank's team quickly found the homeowner and emerged to take him outside and attend to his medical needs with the assistance of two ambulances that had been called in to assist.

The homeowner was totally disoriented but quickly seemed to recover while other firemen made their way to the basement to shut off the generator that was inside. Firemen from the other truck began to set up fans in the basement of the home and implement other safety procedures that they had been trained for.

The gas engine on the generator, of course, was the source of the problem. It had been running all day to provide some electricity. Obviously, it should NOT have been running in the basement. As I sat there, all I really could do was watch. I actually found a set of keys lying on the ground, so I picked them up. A fireman came up to me as I was holding them, and he said, "Wow, you found my keys. Thank you so much. My wife would kill me if I lost these keys."

Several firemen came up to me to thank me for coming to Little Ferry and cooking for everyone. I felt that my contribution was miniscule compared to what I had just witnessed. Here was an assembly of twenty men who had just saved another person's life—but they took the time to thank me. One fireman with tears in his eyes and unable to speak, gave me a hug. The sentiment caused me to feel very small, but I did seem to have been through a "rite of passage" and now had officially bonded with every man on the job.

I was told that the fire chief was in a truck nearby, so I made my way over to him. He greeted me by name as though we had been friends for years. He thanked me for what I had done, and I thanked him for the thrill of a lifetime with the guys in the truck. I asked him if it would be okay to feed the entire department. He said, "No problem." They would get this situation under control within the next thirty minutes, and then everyone could stop by.

We loaded in the behemoth truck and headed back to Mehrhoff. A young man was standing in the back seat area of the fire truck near me, and I asked him, "What makes you want to be a firefighter?" His answer was, "I would rather jump through the roof of a burning fire to save someone's life than have any other job in this country." That testimony revealed the quintessential definition of "serving others" and came out of the mouth of a twenty-two-year-old man, not a twenty-two-year-old kid.

Paradoxically, professional basketball players shoot a leather ball through a net and earn millions of dollars, but the men who surrounded me were saving lives for a fraction of the players' earned interest in their savings accounts! If you or I were awakened by a fireman in the middle of the night to rescue us from a fire in our home, what would the value of our lives be? This thought made me realize that I was, in fact, surrounded by "angels in firemen's apparel."

We made our way home in the fire truck, and at this point, I had been gone at least two hours. It was 8:00 p.m., and a new crowd was coming over to eat. The truck dropped us off as if it were a yellow cab. Everyone who could attend either got out of the truck or had headed to our "soiree" in their own vehicles.

The effect of that run would be added to the collection of memories in my mind that fall into the "life changing" category. Taking "life changing" one step further for me is the prospect of their own death of one for the life of another—a possibility that these men face every day. That would take me months to sort out and think through. The exhilaration of the entire "firemen experience" was an incredible way to end Sunday evening. I won't forget the time that we shared in the truck or my brief opportunity to be part of the team.

So much had happened that I felt the need to find a place to rest or collapse. Lisa handed me something and said, "Eat." Charlotte was now insisting that I find a lounge chair because she was relaxing and wanted everyone to join the crowd around the fire. Mayor Raguseo dropped by to visit with us also. He always knew the latest information on flood insurance issues or homeowner's insurance problems, or updates on other relief efforts.

All of a sudden, things got quiet until Pauley broke the silence and got up and told some jokes. Everyone was exhausted and laughing uncontrollably at times. It didn't matter if the jokes were funny or not because nobody cared. Everyone let go of all the "bad news" and embraced the fun that we could now enjoy together.

Kenny added more jokes by interrupting Pauley, but finally Roy stood up and started pontificating about my "hick" accent. I was surrounded by Italians, and Roy (Swedish) was exercising no restraint in making fun of me. (I was sleeping in his house, so I was fair game.) He was sharing with everyone how he had begun training me to speak "Joisey" and how miserably I had failed to learn from his infinite wisdom.

Roy also mentioned that he was going in the house to make some tai chi with milk and sugar. Brett interrupted and said, "Dad, don't you mean chai tea?" The entire group broke out in laughter, and I was probably laughing the loudest. One guy laughed so hard that he fell out of his chair.

I was so exhausted that I scooted down in my lounge chair, reclined one more notch, and proceeded to listen to the noise around me and focus on the flame of the fire. I wanted to rid my mind of everything but the tip of the flame. The trance that I slipped into did not prevent me from hearing some snickering about getting me into the fire truck and out on the run. Frank was monitoring the volume because he was thoughtful and didn't want me to hear what was being said. They were trying to be respectful and didn't realize that almost anything about me is subject to good-natured banter.

Suddenly, Ryan got up in front of everyone, and with his big voice he could be heard across the street. He had now perfected a new skit about the Hoosier sleeping on the floor of the house. He had mastered my voice and mannerisms. Admittedly, I used the word "unbelievable" many times during my stay in Little Ferry, so Ryan chose a skit to feature not only that word, but now, he was adding the way I walked to his performance. Of course he added extra gestures to be funny. There wasn't a dry eye from laughter in the crowd. Ryan and I had already had many conversations, and I knew that his "impersonation" was a way of showing his love.

Everyone was experiencing total exhaustion, and the crowd was dwindling down to about twenty or fewer people. I might have lasted thirty more minutes until I heard the words from Charlotte, "Hey, let's call it a night." Everyone was weary, and we needed some sleep. We had planned on starting the grill later the following day, like closer to noon.

The house was still fifty-two degrees, and my sleeping bag was still on the living room floor—but it looked like a suite in a hotel to me. I hit the bed and fell asleep immediately only to be awakened by another fire truck later that night. As I lay there, I smiled knowing the exact truck, and I probably knew who was on board, and I also knew how it felt to ride in that truck.

Monday Morning

I awakened to find Roy washing down the driveway with the hose. There had been so many people in the driveway that it needed to be cleaned. Ryan and Brett were offering their assistance as well as moving their personal belongings, and in some cases, parts of the house itself, out of their living areas. Ryan lived in the apartment attached to the house, and Brett lived in the garage, which had been converted into a living space. Drywall, desks, and furniture that had been soaked with flood water had to be removed from both spaces.

Joe showed up and said that Lisa was baking again. He was ready to start the grill whenever we were. We could tell that Monday was winding down with fewer people walking around. By this time, nearly everyone's power had been restored. Even so, we still had people coming over and asking if we had any more pork chops, which we had run out of on Saturday. We cooked some hot dogs between noon and 2:00 p.m. Life was getting more orderly for some although everyone was still dealing with many recovery issues. We finally reached our end to grilling life. We turned off the grill for the last time on Monday afternoon, after having fed nearly 1,700 people! The afternoon was filled with running errands and getting groceries for a special meal that Charlotte wanted to have that night.

Joe and I had an opportunity to be together and actually talk. I realized that my entire time had been spent around lots of people with little time one-on-one with anybody, except for a few brief moments spent with Roy, Charlotte, and Ryan. Charlotte and Roy's house now had the lights back on with trusted work from the in-house electricians, but there was still no heat because of the damage to the system. This made the house feel more normal and allowed us to use the kitchen.

I was still unwinding from the miraculous and exhausting days, and more exhaustion was to come. The evening ended at dinner with several people who had worked closest with us and a few other volunteers who wanted to stay and enjoy the time together. It was a fun evening filled with laughter and no discussion of the damage and problems that Sandy had caused.

Tuesday Morning

I was up early with Mattie's familiar little sniff-sniff and lick on my cheek. I am not sure about others, but for me, a lick on the edge of my face has more waking value than a blaring alarm clock. She didn't want to sleep with me, and she didn't want me to sleep any longer. I wasn't ready to go outside, but she was so I took her. The fall air was quite chilly, but it was a beautiful morning with sunshine and a scent of salty sea air.

Mattie and I went to the backyard for her needs and then back in the house. Roy was up next with activities aimed at cleaning up and working in his basement. Several water-logged items still had to be removed, and he needed help. I volunteered to assist him but was always and kindly told, "No, thank you." My job was over, and Roy had Brett and Ryan to help with basement activities.

I got myself together and headed down to Joe and Lisa's house for a hot shower. As I walked through the door, Lisa had the kitchen smelling like breakfast. The scent of fresh-baked goods, which was now the norm, filled the air. Lisa's theory was that if she cooked, it helped heat their home. I was refreshed from getting a better night's sleep and enthused about everything, including breakfast. Since it would still be a while before we could eat, I headed back down to Charlotte's house.

On the way back, Patty stuck her head out the door and yelled at me. "Hey, coffee is brewing, are you ready for a cup?" I did not hesitate and promptly walked through their door. Marty and Patty were good friends with Joe because of a work relationship between Marty and Joe. Marty and I talked about cars. He is a master mechanic and has an incredible memory for car parts.

Patty and he had been married a long time, and they had a daughter who was involved with several community activities including volunteering at the Boy's Club. It was fun to decompress and just listen, but I was struggling with the idea of leaving. So many things had happened to me that I was unprepared for.

I enjoyed visiting and doing absolutely nothing. Patty offered their couch, food, and even their bed to me if I needed it. I must have stayed an hour or more because my phone started ringing. Lisa was wondering where I was because she had called Charlotte to see if I was at their home. Charlotte had called me to see if I was still at Joe and Lisa's home. I was physically located between the two homes. So I said my goodbyes and headed back to Lisa's house for breakfast.

I still wasn't ready to pack anything including the grill that I brought or any other supplies. I even seemed rebellious about the thought of leaving my beloved Little Ferry. Several calls from people in the community saying goodbye were a reminder that it was time to go. Their collective outpouring of affection was clear to me that I was part of their family also.

As I left, I smiled all the way back to Charlotte's house. When I returned to the familiar driveway, a guest who was like family to Charlotte was visiting her. He was a robust gentleman, about seventy-five or so, and he was sharing information about the Medicare supplement insurance that he had. Since I have experience in the insurance business, I talked to him about his situation and tried to offer information that might help him make a decision on the type of coverage to best suit his needs. We visited for a while, and he returned to his home not far away.

I started to gather personal items, most of which had been misplaced or displaced. I was not gung ho, but I did make an effort on this final day to collect all the things that I had brought. Later in the afternoon, Joe and I returned to the store and bought the items needed to make a last dinner for all of us along with some of the volunteers who were coming over. I tried to assist in the making of the meal but was turned away again.

The entire evening was a night to remember with smells of bread and garlic to Italian sauces and pasta. Funny stories that had already been told, as well as many we had not heard, were shared throughout the evening with laughter—which was roaring at times. Everyone took pot shots and joked about each other. I was not exempt from Ryan's theatrical efforts to show everyone how he could sound like me and talk like me again, and of course, everyone rolled. It took my mind off returning home and made for a perfect evening enjoyed with my New Jersey family.

Wednesday Morning

My day began early and I moved slowly. This may have been the most difficult morning, marking my departure from this place and my life-changing experiences. I would not let my mind wander beyond what I had to do to get ready to go. I got up before

Mattie could greet me, and I walked outside. It was sunny, but with the chilly wind, a jacket was required. The familiar saltwater scent in the air was invigorating. I walked out of the driveway and headed down Mehrhof toward the shower at Joe and Lisa's home.

A Little Ferry city truck was headed down the street, and the truck driver honked the horn and acted like he was going to hit me. A big guy driving the truck was laughing loudly and stopped and talked with me. He had stopped by for something to eat earlier in the week. We said our last goodbyes, and down the street I went.

I had called Lisa earlier to see if they were up, and her standard answer was "Yes, and the coffee is ready." I was warmly greeted, and the aroma of a great coffee blend filled the air. These would be our last hours together, but it didn't feel too bad because they all knew that I was missed at home. Under the surface, we all knew that we had experienced something special, and that parting would be more than difficult.

After my shower I told Joe and Lisa that I would like to take them to breakfast with Charlotte and Roy. Lisa always knew where everything was for me. She didn't know me BLF (Before Little Ferry), but she knew that I had a problem keeping up with everything from my billfold to my cellphone and other items between. As I left their home, Lisa was running through the check list with me: billfold, glasses, cell phone, brain.

The last trip back down Mehrhof felt strange but not final. When I returned, my truck was mostly loaded with the gear that I had brought. Roy and I went to the garage to figure out what I had forgotten, if anything. A shovel, a chain saw, my clothes, and I was nearly ready to go. I went in the house and talked with Charlotte. We were all going to meet Lisa and Joe, but Charlotte said that if we could meet them an hour later, it would give her time to tell me a little more about her family's history in Little Ferry and show me some things in the area that I had missed.

As Charlotte and I walked out, Roy was dealing with more water-logged items in the basement, and he was not going to be able to go with us. After loading my final items, I looked at Roy and felt my body shake as though the temperature had turned frigid. I walked over and hugged him—we could say very little. He could only say, "I love you," and I returned the sentiment. I said goodbye to Ryan and Brett also, and a minute later Charlotte and I were out of the driveway in my truck.

We toured the area where damage was so obvious. Within two blocks, a large tree had blown over and ripped up half of the sidewalk with it as it fell. When the tree landed, it hit two homes at once. We drove down Mehrhof toward the Meadowlands and the marshy areas and then toward the Izod Center. The stadium was huge and was located for easy access from I-95 or the Pennsylvania Turnpike. We drove into the parking lot, I took some pictures, and we turned around and headed for a local restaurant.

Joe and Lisa met us, and we found a booth. The service was slow because there were so many people in the restaurant. Most people had regained electricity, but not everyone had hot water, so dealing with clean dishes and cookware was creating problems that contributed to the crowd.

The conversation was a continuation of getting to know each other. I had some pictures of our kids in my phone that I showed them. I also had pictures of our home and other "things" in my life, but somehow, that did not seem appropriate after the damage that had dominated our lives for the last five days.

As I finished I said, "Do you guys want to tell me the best way to get on the turnpike, or do you want to lead me to the correct highway?" Joe almost jumped up from the table. He said, "What are you talking about?" I said, "I mean that I am ready to go, and I am leaving." Joe was almost mad, sad, and astonished all at the same time. He could not believe that I was leaving to go home after breakfast. He hardly said another word and sat there stunned. Lisa was driving her Jeep, and we agreed that she would lead me to the highway. We all got up and walked outside and said goodbye.

The emotional energy could have been cut with a knife. We all really dreaded this moment. I made my exit as brief as possible and then jumped into my truck, and they got into Lisa's Jeep. I followed them to the Pennsylvania Turnpike. Once we arrived at my exit, Lisa turned her turn signal on, which meant that was the exit to take.

THE JOURNEY HOME

The silence in my truck was deafening. I just realized that I had not stopped moving, cooking, talking, working, and thinking for five days solid. I was actually alone and just starting to take inventory within myself. I knew that these events had changed me, and the difference was so profound that I felt overloaded.

There was too much of everything to remember and no way of discerning any specific thing. I needed to pay attention to my driving, try to stay safe, and keep moving down the road. I made it one hour and noticed a rest stop that I was unable to avoid. I was so sleepy and exhausted and was near falling asleep.

I soon exited into the "Cars Only" area and found a space immediately. As I drove into the parking place, I didn't even pull all the way forward, but I did have the sense to push down on the emergency brake to stop the truck before contacting the curb with my front tires. I had never used the emergency brake like that, and that was all I remembered for the next hour. I passed out with the truck three feet from the curb, the door half open, and my seat reclined.

When I woke up, there were several cars in the parking lot and people moving to and from their cars. The car next to my truck had two kids who were pointing at me and laughing. I am sure that was a funny sight, but I was so exhausted that I failed to appreciate the humor. It reminded me of my uncle's saying: "If you are ever in doubt whether to laugh at me or laugh with me, laugh at me; it will be good for both of us." After a few minutes of stretching, walking outdoors, and a cup of coffee, I was ready to go.

My trip home to Indiana was filled with many telephone calls. Most of the next few hours were spent talking with people I had just spent the last five days with. Joe called first and told me that when Lisa led me to the exit, they pulled their Jeep over into the emergency lane and "cried their eyes out just like babies." We laughed about that, now that we could.

I received a touching call from a man who started the conversation by saying that his name was not important because I would not remember him. "I wanted to call and thank you for what you did for everyone but especially for me. I went over and you guys fed me two times, but I did not introduce myself to anyone."

"My world had been horrible, and then the storm came. I have struggled with several vices in my life, which led me to consider suicide. I was so inspired by your visit and the response from people wanting to help that I have made some big changes in my life. My entire faith in humanity has been restored because of what happened."

I thanked him for the kind words and answered him by saying, "I may have brought a match, but you guys started the fire. Thank you for your story, and I am so glad that you called me." I glowed after the call. No radio, eyes on the road, seventy mph, and I was feeling so humbled by what he had said. I realized that his appreciation was for everyone that had been part of our efforts. Limitless joy seemed to permeate my reality.

My next call was from Nancy. She was from a nearby city, and she had visited us on three occasions. Nancy and I had become friends, and she also donated some items for us to give away. She called for two reasons. First, she called to suggest that I spend the night in a motel on the way home—she knew I was wiped out and wanted to make sure I was safe on the way home.

Second, she also had a story to tell me about a guy she went to high school with who had also stopped by for a bite to eat while we were cooking, and she knew that I would remember him. She said they had a very difficult relationship when they were younger. She had always struggled with painful memories from that time.

She proceeded to read an email that he had sent to her apologizing for some mistakes he had made and asking her forgiveness for having been offensive. She was so moved by his email, which made her cry, that she wanted to share it with me. She felt that the storm had influenced his life but that it was my visit to Little Ferry that changed his life and prompted his email and apology.

I thanked her for her kindness, but I couldn't take credit for the change. I came to Little Ferry because I felt led there, and there was nothing else I could have done. We talked a few more minutes before saying goodbye. After disconnecting, I experienced that complete joy again. The call hit me, and I wept, which further strengthened how grateful I was to have been placed into a part of something that was so much more than just a response to a disaster.

The next call was from Allen. He also had been with us every day and offered to help serve or cook several times. He wanted to check on me and my trip back home. He also wanted to know when I was coming back. His experience with us had a major impact on his life that he wanted to talk about.

He said, "I am not a religious man at all. I was not raised in a church, and my parents did not expect me to go to church. I have been married for several years. We have a son who is three now, and we recently found a home that suited us, so we bought it, thinking we did the right thing. We signed the papers on October 2, 2012, and we were supposed to take possession of the home on November 1.

"The storm has delayed the 'American Dream' for us. Five feet of water and saturated drywall will require the house to get rehabilitated, and it might be months before we can move in." He said he felt cheated and violated, but he also felt something different that he had not felt before.

He wanted me to know that his personal change was his attitude about church and, more importantly, people who go to church. (I had never discussed church with Allen.) "I have been so moved by you coming up here that I felt encouraged to tell you that when this life is all over, I will see you at the Pearly Gates!"

I said that I appreciated the benefit of the doubt that "I" would be at the Pearly Gates to meet him, but his conversion was awe inspiring! He continued to credit me with changes in his life. I told him that "I" was not the source of the change. I was moved to tears and had difficulty saying goodbye to this young man and his powerful testimony. Again, complete joy overwhelmed me. I sat there driving, but my heart said, "Thank you" to God for letting me be a part of what had happened—whatever it was.

Pennsylvania had turned into Ohio, and evening was rapidly approaching. I still had two more hours before getting into Columbus. I would be lucky to make it that long before falling asleep.

My phone was quiet for thirty minutes, and then Charlotte checked on me. She wanted to make sure that I was going to stop on the way home and get some rest. She said that a woman named Meredith, a friend of hers, had called her. Meredith had been raised in the Catholic Church. Three years ago, she had some incredible bad luck and felt that God had left her, and she was angry about it. She had no intention of ever going to church again.

Meredith had come over several times to visit while we were cooking and help out if we needed her because she didn't live too far away. She was so moved with all that had happened to her, and she was calling to let Charlotte know that she would be in church on Sunday morning. She was actually excited about the idea of going and wanted us to know it. Again, this call was revealing the life changing events in others while I was trying to understand the changes in my own life.

I received another call from Bruce. He wanted to tell me that he had cleared his schedule and was ready to return to Little Ferry with me on Saturday morning after an obligation that he had at his church. He could stay for three days, which would be long enough considering the work he wanted to do—clean muck out of homes filled with sand and water. Since I had already met the UMCOR representative for the Bergen County area, a follow-up conversation with him would help Bruce get to the type of place he was seeking.

I was excited about this, so I called Joe and asked him to contact the fire chief to see if we could do an appreciation dinner for the first responders and invite the firemen, ambulance employees, and police to come over to the firehouse for a grilled meal. Hopefully, we could use the Marshal Street location, which was central for most people.

We could start late on Sunday afternoon and have activities for the kids, so families could come over and be together. He thought that was a great idea, and Lisa knew someone who was available for face painting and games that kids could play. Joe would take care of it tomorrow and let me know. I knew that Bruce would help me on Sunday, and having someone else in the car would make a return trip much easier.

I approached the exit for Columbus and found a Bob Evans restaurant and stopped there. After eating, I knew that I would not be able to stay awake and drive. I found a motel near the exit and pulled in. I remember getting in the room, and that was it. I got up early the next morning and was soon looking for coffee. I was about six hours from home and needed to stay focused.

Thursday Morning

I took 71 South and moved toward Indiana. I was beginning to remember some things from my visit that replayed in my mind like a video. I seemed to be recalling with more clarity, now, the things that I had experienced, especially on Saturday.

I was so excited to tell anyone about what had happened and could hardly think about anything else. The last several hours of the trip were spent quietly driving—and feeling very thankful. I really struggled to think beyond getting home. I stayed calm and drove without a radio. I felt like a "different" person feeling joy at the highest level that I was capable. I felt so detached from the person I had been and was struggling to learn more about the person I was becoming. If my previous life had ended with any unfinished items on my "bucket list," it just wouldn't matter anymore.

Susan called to check my progress and told me that we had been invited to go to dinner with our cousins on Friday night. There was a ring of excitement in her voice. I was approaching the exit for Louisville, Kentucky, and that was an indication that I was close to home. She was relieved that I was getting closer to Indiana, but she would be late getting home from work. As I made my way onto I-64, I had less than two hours of driving left.

Joe called and confirmed that our meal for the first responders was set for Sunday afternoon, and a nice grill at the firehouse would be available. The fire chief made the arrangements, and everything would be ready to go when we got back to Little Ferry. Wow, that was only three days away, and I had not shared the good news with Susan. For the next one hundred miles my phone remained quiet. It was nice to begin the process of decompression, but that would not last long since so much awaited me, and I needed to get home to prepare for the return trip.

As I entered our rock driveway, everything looked different. The trees seemed to have changed as well as the driveway itself. As I drove in, three deer were crossing the driveway. My heart was pounding with excitement, and my anticipation was building as Sophie and Alfie, our two miniature dachshunds, would likely be barking and waiting for me at the door.

I pulled in the driveway, and the first things I saw were the two little heads, barking in a duet, with noses pressed against the glass of the front door. All I could hear was barking out of these "angels" as their mother (Susan) affectionately refers to them. After a substantial amount of face licking, they allowed me to come into the house, but their behavior was the first witness to me that I was different and they knew it. I walked into a space that was almost foreign to me.

RECONNECTING

The second I crossed the threshold, I noticed that the smell, look, and feel, of our home had changed. Perhaps more accurately, my perception of our home had changed. It felt as though I was visiting the home of a good friend who had moved to another location. I slowly walked around the inside of the house. I went to the living room and circled around the two sofas as though I was doing a victory lap. That evoked total nostalgia where eight days earlier I had paced around the same two sofas at 4:15 a.m. with a burning in my heart that "surpassed all understanding."

The dogs' instincts were keen, and that affected their behavior toward me. They sat on the edge of the stairway and stared at every move I made. With their heads synchronized, they watched from left to right as I walked around the stairway. They were not scared, they were just aware that, "Dang, Dad seems different."

I walked into the kitchen and stood still as I looked out the window without moving for about forty-five minutes. Just complete silence and no interference. Although my body was motionless as I gazed out into the woods, my mind was swirling. The enormity of what I had been through was just beginning to sink in. I couldn't really begin to grasp all that had happened. The time span of forty-five minutes became two hours quickly. I didn't unload the truck, and all I could do was stand and stare. Sophie and Alfie gave up on watching me and decided to go back to their bed.

I finally heard the familiar sound of a car coming down the driveway, and the dogs started barking their heads off. I had forgotten how shrill and loud Sophie's voice was. Our wood floors seemed to echo the intense volume. They were anxious because their Mommy was home. Alfie, in his excitement, always needs a ball to be thrown outside, and Sophie visits long enough to go outside and relieve herself and then, back to bed.

I opened the front door to let the dogs out, and I stepped outside to be warmly greeted by the most incredible woman. She had been my sounding board, tactical officer, spiritual adviser, and coach all at the same time since I had left one week and one day ago. She knew everything about the trip, and she has been the other half of me for more than twenty years.

The embrace was familiar but also a reminder of how different I felt inside. Everything felt different, and so did she, in an amazing, wonderful way. We went into the house and talked very little. Most of what happened had already been spoken about, so we didn't need to repeat it. She went about her business, and I stood near a window and said nothing.

The television was on, and I didn't pay any attention to what was said. I had heard very little news in the previous week and didn't care about any news now. As I stared into space, I was reviewing videos in my mind and still could hardly believe what had happened. I could not have a continuing thought of anything and I was dazed. So the noise in the house became something that was just noise; the noise inside my head became dull and silent until my body said, "I need some sleep."

Alfie started groaning and making soft whimpering sounds at Susan. That is how he lets her know that he is ready to go to bed. When she ignores him, he turns up the volume by barking. That means, "Hey I want to go to bed now, and I want you to go with me."

We had both been through a lot of emotions, and it was time to rest. Susan had put fresh sheets on the bed, and she and the dogs went to bed ahead of me. When I walked up the stairs, the dogs started barking at me like I was an intruder. This is their normal behavior and is a mix of excitement and annoyance, and they don't settle down until I make it to bed. The bed felt new to me as did everything else. Sleeping can sometimes be a challenge, but it wasn't that night.

Friday Morning

The next thing I remembered was hearing the shower running at 5:00 a.m. I was ready to get up anyway since I had gotten used to Eastern Time. I got up and still felt some stress in my shoulders that had previously filled my entire body. Susan needed to be at the office early, so she reminded me that we were going out for dinner around 6:00 p.m.

After she left for the office, I was really excited to go to the church office to see Pastors Steve and Chris. I hurried to get ready, hoping I could see them both. Their schedules are always jammed and packed to the brim. The moment that I walked into the office, I could feel high energy in the air. I was warmly greeted and embraced by everyone in the church office. I saw a few of my friends in the hallways. They shared kind words and recognition of how "radical" making the trip to New Jersey was.

CONFESSIONS OF THE MIRACULOUS

Suddenly I noticed Pastor Steve was standing in his office doorway with a huge smile, and he seemed so excited about my return. He hugged me like a brother, and his energy always exudes love and is love. He started to shut the door behind me, and Chris walked in. His embrace was robust and energetic. He was eager to hear what had happened. I was not prepared for the challenge of describing the stories without getting emotional and breaking down. That felt a bit embarrassing but was an obvious sign that I had experienced something so powerful that words escaped me and emotions engulfed me.

As I began to explain what had happened, I sensed the power of the story and started to recognize that everything I was saying was about me. That immediately caused concern because the story was more complex than that. Also, I didn't go to New Jersey with the idea that there would be any story, but certainly not one about me.

The conversation changed when I mentioned that Bruce had called me and I was going back to Little Ferry with him and would be leaving the next day. Steve instinctively knew that it was time for prayer, and he was seated directly in front of me with my hands in his.

Chris got behind me and put his hands on my shoulders. I remember two things from when he touched me: His hands felt unusually warm, feeling almost like I had a sunburn, and my body shook as though I had chills when Steve started to pray. The energy of the prayer felt like electricity passing through me. We concluded our meeting and went our separate ways.

I began to feel disappointed when I left and returned home. I went into the living room, got on my knees, and prayed that God would strip me of ego and pride about any aspect of the trip—and that in any future conversations about the trip, I would be humble and mindful of the listener. I arose with the hope that my prayers would be answered.

I then made several calls for some pending business and found that it was difficult to focus on work. The conversations soon turned to the storm, and I appreciated the interest many people showed in those affected by Sandy and the trip to New Jersey to help them. They had seen the information in the newspaper or on television. I became excited to start talking about some of the experiences and the wonderful people I had met in Little Ferry. This reminded me that we would soon be preparing to return to Little Ferry and that I would be better able to tend to business in Evansville when I got back.

DEVONA—ILLUMINATING THE PATH FOR CHILDREN

A very important personal call that I made was to Devona, a close friend of the family. She had been my Sunday School teacher when I was a child, and she continues to devote her Sunday mornings to teaching preschool children. One of my earliest memories is that she gave me a small cross that glowed in the dark. One side was inscribed with "God is Love," and the other side read, "Love is God." I used to lie in bed at night and hold a flashlight close to the cross for about ten seconds. Then the cross would glow for about thirty minutes as I went to sleep.

Devona had read about the New Jersey trip and mailed a postcard with an inspirational message that I read several times before contacting her. She was elated that I called, and I could feel smiling, laughter, and joy as she heard about the event in Little Ferry.

She credited all things to the glory of God, which is her rock and foundation. The only time she would interrupt me was when she would say, "Amen, hallelujah, or praise God!"

She was the inspiration that I needed at that moment. I felt empowered and resolute from our conversation, which confirmed what she believed was God's plan and how He set up the trip and the lives that had interwoven with mine. Her summation was interesting to the point of saying things about my experiences that I didn't even know. Of course, she spoke about my parents, who have been gone for several years, and said they would have been happy about what happened to us.

I told her that I felt and heard the presence of my late mother more than once during the trip. There are many things that we are left with from parents that live on in our hearts. My choice is to remember all things that were inspirational and honor their lives. My parents were my friends, and we shared years of music, laughter, travel, and family gatherings.

After the call, I walked out of the house and took a walk through the woods. I found a tree and hugged it for several minutes as I was so grateful for the privilege. Susan hugged trees once in a while, and she had talked me into doing the same thing. I usually made fun of her for doing it but, on this occasion, changed my attitude about it as I felt the life within that tree that God provides us. My dad was the only other person I had ever seen hug a tree, so I suppose he knew something about that too.

I went back into the house and started making notes about my trip and especially the events on Saturday. I wanted to jot everything down while it was fresh in my mind. Susan and I were going to dinner, and I had a short time left to get some paperwork done. The time passed quickly, and more barking from the dogs indicated their "mommy" was coming down the driveway again.

I knew that I needed to deliver the bad news (as it were) that Bruce had called and we were planning on returning the next day. Yikes! So when she came in and took the dogs out, I was ready for her with a story that would blame Bruce and hold myself blameless. I told her that Bruce felt so badly that he had to tell me no (when I invited him to go the first time) that he called me and wanted to go to Little Ferry but Anne (his wife) couldn't make the trip, so he was just wondering if it would be okay if I make the return trip.

She giggled and said, "So Anne can't make it, huh?" She knew Bruce, and she knows me and said, "Okay, like I am going to say no to such a carefully crafted story as that? Go!" I immediately called Bruce and told him the great news!

We were picked up by our cousins around 7:00 p.m. and headed to a nearby restaurant. My head was swirling at dinner, and the thought of food was beyond my interest, but I needed something to eat. By about 8:15, my stomach was upset after eating. I had to leave the table twice. It had been days since I had eaten a real meal, and it would take a while to readjust to regular food. Susan handled most of the conversation at dinner, and there was little discussion about New Jersey. We got home and went to bed immediately with the dogs leading the way.

Saturday Morning

The night seemed short, and I awakened early and thought about what needed to be done to get ready to leave again. I was looking forward to going back and spending time on the road with Bruce. My phone rang at 8:00 a.m. and it was Bruce. His voice sounded like someone had died. He said that he and Anne had gone to dinner the night before and something made him sick. He was so sick, in fact, that he nearly passed out before they left the restaurant. He felt that food poisoning was most likely the problem. He was very sorry, but he needed at least three hours to figure out if he could even make the trip.

I fell into a void with nothing to say when we ended the call. I would hang on to every minute for the next three hours. My phone rang about fifteen minutes later, and it was Bruce. He said that it was unfair for me to delay my plans to wait on his decision. He also said, "You know me, and I would not back out of this trip unless I felt like I was on my death bed, and that is exactly how I feel. I just can't make it. You deserve to know now, and I don't want to put you off. I am really sorry." The reality was that traveling with his condition would be extremely hard on him and probably require many stops and/or a return trip home—which would not help those we both wanted to help.

I went downstairs and took a shower and began to wonder why this was happening. I got through the shower and accepted that I was going to return alone. Instinctively, I sent a text to the men in my Bible study group that meets at the Donut Bank on Thursdays at 6:00 a.m. I told them that Bruce was very sick, and because of my promise to return to Little Ferry, I had no other choice but to go back alone.

I needed to get the oil changed in the truck and drove to the east side of town to get that taken care of. I had to sit in a line for about thirty minutes and wait. I didn't care because of needing to rest. I was now dreading another thirty hours (round trip) of driving alone behind the wheel. I gazed out the window without really seeing anything.

A short time later, I received a call from Blaine, one of the guys from the Thursday morning group. He had received my text explaining that I was going back to Little Ferry by myself. He was thinking about returning with me and wondered if he could bring his twelve-year-old son, Jonathan. I had no problem with any part of that. My hope was that a twelve-year-old wouldn't become bored on a trip like this, but I was excited about the possibility of someone else going. I knew it wasn't smart to go alone.

When I got home, I received a call confirming that Blaine and Jonathan were going! We would leave by 5:00 p.m. I asked him to go by Dewig Meats and pick up the second food donation that they offered us. This time we took bratwurst and hot dogs. We had two huge boxes, and we had enough food for 500 people. My clothes were packed by Susan since she had agreed that it was important for me to return. She and I said our goodbyes as she was leaving to attend an event in a nearby town.

THE RETURN TRIP

Blaine showed up with his wife, Shannon, and Jonathan. I took one look at Jonathan and instinctively knew he was supposed to be there. Blaine came over to me as I was loading the truck and said, "I want to introduce you to your mini-me." Jonathan had been working on his Joisey accent and stuck out his hand and said, "HOW YOOOOU DOOOOIN?" We bonded in a New Jersey second.

His appearance was so similar to my own at age twelve. I was amazed. Jonathan was at that difficult age of early adolescence, but you would never know it by his demeanor. He was outspoken, outgoing, and self-assured with an intellectual charm. His quick wit and timing seemed to put him way beyond his years. My blessing was the responsibility to influence the life of this young man. Learning to sacrifice for someone else was a great way to do that in my opinion.

Blaine found a quiet moment with me alone as we gathered supplies. He shared that "our" trip was an answered prayer for him, and the timing was perfect—it was exactly what he and Jonathan really needed. I told him that "they" were the answered prayer for me.

We quickly finished loading coolers and supplies, and Blaine huddled us together to pray for God's blessing on our trip. We quickly said goodbye to Shannon, and out the driveway we went. I-64 was ten minutes away, and I was not driving. Blaine was in charge, and I could visit and relax. He probably saved my life by driving.

Susan called as we made our way onto I-64 and asked to speak with Blaine. I handed him the phone, and his side of the conversation went silent. Blaine was careful not to reveal the content of their conversation, and I figured if Susan wanted me to know something, she would have told me.

RECALLING MY FIRST "MISSION" TRIP

As we approached exit 79, I pointed out a house on the north side of I-64 to Jonathan. I explained to him that my first "mission trip" at age twelve was to help build that house with my family. My grandfather, or "Pop," as everyone called him, had a brother, "Uncle S," who lost his home to a fire in the mid-1960s.

When Pop received the call about the fire, he sprang into action and started planning immediately. He got on the phone and called my dad and my four uncles and told everyone about what had happened. He also said that "we" (meaning if you answered the phone, you were part of the "we") were going to help build Uncle S a new home. His goal was to be "under roof" in three weekends. "Gather your saws, hammers, squares, and tools, and meet us at the farm and we will travel together in a caravan. We are leaving the house at 6:30 on Saturday morning."

Some thought he was crazy, and others made no comment because Pop had the last word, especially if you were married to one of his daughters. Nobody could or ever would tell Pop "no." My grandmother called my mom and aunts and started meal planning for our "mission." All of my aunts came together to help prepare the meals needed while working for this shared goal.

I remembered what an amazing experience it was to watch everyone come together for one common purpose. It was more than a commission; it was an obvious "mission of love." Our crew consisted of ten people in my family and five men from Uncle S's family who worked together for three weekends in a row. I helped as much as I could to raise walls and roof the home in that period of time.

The house was under roof and out of the cold on the third weekend! It was Pop's sheer will and determination that made that happen. He and my grandmother both had stubborn but generous spirits. Pop said, "I am a Dutchman and a farmer, and that is all I will ever be. Everyone makes fun of the farmers, but try to eat food without us. Who do you think puts food on the table?"

Interestingly, Pop's barn had burned in 1959. Uncle S brought a crew of his four sons down to help rebuild Pop's barn. In that instance, the poles were set with tractors and the roof was on in one weekend.

It was so exciting to be a part of those projects. It was great to be part of a family who reached out in that way and now to have an opportunity to share the stories. Jonathan, listening intently, was sitting right behind me with his face tucked between the front seats to be a part of our conversation. I remembered sitting the exact same way when I was his age.

The nostalgia of the moment caused me to be very sensitive to Jonathan's experience because I realized it would stay with him forever. There may be a day that he does his own mission with a young teenager looking to him to learn these principles of service. I knew that Blaine and Jonathan were not with me by accident.

We made it through Louisville and headed for Cincinnati. Jonathan was hungry, and we discussed barbeque, so we stopped at a great place and had fun in a restaurant about thirty miles north of town. The rest of the night would be dedicated to driving, which would be necessary to reach Little Ferry in the morning. For obvious reasons, I loved going back. There was much about this trip that felt like traveling to visit family.

We talked into the night until Blaine convinced me to trade seats with Jonathan and rest in the back seat. I kept asking him to let me drive, but he would not consider it. He said, "Look, I don't know what jobs I'll have when we get there, but I know that the most important job right now is driving—and I am not going to stop until we get there. His statement had the sound of determination from another place. Susan must have said something that influenced his thinking.

I had not slept soundly since I left for New Jersey the first time. I finally kept quiet and fell asleep in the back seat of the truck. I had never been in the back seat of the truck, but it was fairly comfortable so I finally rested. A few hours passed and we needed gas, so we stopped briefly. We were getting close to Little Ferry, so I talked Blaine into letting me drive to give him a break from driving all night. We were within three hours of our destination.

We arrived in Little Ferry around 8:00 a.m., and Joe and Lisa had left the key in the mailbox so we could get in. We walked upstairs and entered their home, and the entire place was filled with aroma of Lisa's great coffee. As we walked through the door, it was like a family reunion. Lisa was in the kitchen, and Joe was at the table working with food for some dish he was making. Lisa had baked sweet rolls, and the scent would make anyone hungry for breakfast. She had also baked an egg and bacon casserole breakfast, the aroma of which was also filling the air. We visited briefly, and I introduced everyone. Laughter filled the air in a short time.

I felt the need to walk down Mehrhof to check in with Roy and Charlotte and let them know that we had arrived safely. The walk was only a few minutes away, and the morning air was brisk and invigorating. It was so exciting to be back where I had experienced the life changing events, and how lucky I was to be walking down this street again. It was almost as though I had never left.

On my way, I encountered a woman who was carrying some wet clothing. She was likely beyond her mid-seventies, and she looked exhausted. When I spoke to her, she stopped walking and started a conversation about the damage that her home had suffered. Her daughter lived nearby, and she was headed there to dry the clothing that she was carrying. Like most people with basements, she had lost the furnace for her home as well as everything that was being stored in the basement. It seemed like she really needed someone to talk with, and she was very friendly. She said that the electricity might be back on, but it would be a long time before much else was back to normal, if ever.

As I continued down the street, everything that had happened seemed to hit me all at once: the timing of arriving in Little Ferry; turning down Mehrhof; the guy with the chicken; Roy and Charlotte's home; the personal encounters with all of the people; all the donations; the incredible journey, and all of the other unexpected events. Could I really have been part of something that was larger than grilling food?

Susan called about that time to check on me, and I wasn't sounding too great because of being a bit overwhelmed with emotion. I stopped to talk with her and hopefully collect my thoughts. I told her about everything hitting me, which was complicated by the fact that we had driven all night and I hadn't gotten much sleep. Her first words after I explained were: "You don't seem to be grounded." (These were the same words that Pastor Jeff had spoken one week earlier.) Her conversation was a breath of fresh air as she encouraged me to collect myself for the day. She knew that we had a big meal to fix for the first responders, and I would encounter many of the people I had met. I felt relieved and continue walking down the familiar driveway to say hi to Charlotte and the family.

Everyone was inside, and we were so excited to see each other again so soon. As we were talking, my phone vibrated with a text from Susan. I glanced at it quickly and it said, "Remember to breathe." I replied, "We are living on air from God today." I received another text about ten minutes later but didn't look at it.

I talked with Charlotte while Roy and Ryan returned to the basement to remove more personal items soaked with seawater. All of the electrical breakers had been restored and the electricity was on, but the heating systems were still not working.

A short time later, we all went outside because Lisa, Joe, Blaine, and Jonathan were on the way over so everyone could meet each other. The minute that Jonathan opened the door of Lisa's Jeep, he shook hands with Roy and with a loud voice in Jersey style said, "HOW YOOOOU DOOOOIN?" Everyone broke out in laughter, and that was the last time that Jonathan was a stranger to anyone who would meet him. He could handle the spotlight and being the center of attention with no problems. Bashful was not in his dictionary, and energy was his middle name. I could tell immediately that he would remain the comedian.

Lisa and Joe had invited Blaine, Jonathan, and me to attend the church service at the Tenafly United Methodist Church—where I had attended church the prior Sunday. So Blaine, Jonathan, and I got in my truck and followed Joe and Lisa to church. I was driving and suddenly felt extremely sleepy. We were three blocks from the church, and at the stop sign, I fell asleep for about thirty seconds. Blaine saw it and jokingly said, "Do I need to drive and we are only three blocks away? You have to be kidding me." Jonathan chimed in with his giggles and comments. The laughing woke me up, so I was fine to drive the rest of the way.

We walked through the door of the church and were warmly greeted by everyone. I recognized many of the folks, and others reminded me that we had met last week. Everyone was genuinely happy to be at church and ready for the new day. We stayed busy with introductions and getting reacquainted. Reverend Beth was the next cheerful face we saw. She met us but was very busy with last-minute preparations before her message. Choir members were busy with rehearsing early. Blaine and Jonathan walked around and greeted people as if they had been members for several years.

As the service began, we were introduced by Reverend Beth. As she began her message of "Serving and Helping Others," she began to show the pictures she had taken the previous Sunday in Charlotte's driveway. She used the activity as an example of serving others: the tables full of food and donations, people cooking food, others posing for a picture, laughter, and the evidence of everyone at work provided good material for her sermon. Her message was powerful and filled with the benefits we receive by helping others and a reminder that we are all called to do so.

She concluded her message and again introduced the regional coordinator of the United Methodist Committee on Relief, who is a member of the church. He stood up and spoke briefly about the United Methodist efforts to address the damage from Sandy and more specifically, on the Jersey shoreline. Reverend Beth closed with a final prayer, and everyone moved about and most of the members headed for the social hour that included the post-service meal.

I felt the need for us to get back and start working on the dinner and activities that we were preparing for the first responders and their families. We had a lot to do. Lisa was coordinating the meal with Charlotte to decide what extra food would be needed to go with the meat that we brought from Dewig's back in Indiana.

As we made our way back to Roy and Charlotte's house to get ready for the day, my phone rang and Susan wondered if I had read her text that she sent earlier. I asked if she meant, "Remember to breathe?" (which I had already responded to with the message: "We are living on air from God today."). She said, "No, I am talking about my response to your text." I said "No," so she abruptly said, "Read it." Then she hung up the phone without saying anything else. I thought that was the strangest call from her that I had ever received. When we arrived at Charlotte's house, I sat in the driveway and carefully reviewed the three exchanged texts. They are in order and verbatim:

Susan: Remember to Breathe. (strange for her to say)

Me: We are living on air from God today. (strange for me to say back)

Susan: Then breathe a lot. Be like a tree. Roots (feet) planted firmly in the ground with Branches (arms) reaching upward. Draw your strength from Mother Earth and Father God. (off the chart strange)

I was still sitting in the truck alone and I said, rather loudly, "You've got to be kidding me. Be like a tree? What are you talking about?" I left the truck without thinking of that text again.

Jonathan had gone to find Roy and Ryan. They immediately put Jonathan to work, which made him very happy. Lisa and Joe showed up a short time later, so things began to happen in a hurry. We had plenty of food, and we could serve 300 if everyone showed up.

Considerable time was spent loading the trays and trays of baked goods that Lisa brought and the supplies that were left from the food donations from the prior weekend. The caravan of three vehicles left the driveway with everyone involved, and we drove the short distance to the fire house, ready to serve.

As soon as we arrived, several firemen and their families were already working to set up chairs and tables. The weather on Sunday afternoon was perfect. Brisk winds from the water less than a mile away and cool fall temperatures, absent of all humidity, combined with an abundance of beautiful sunshine gave everyone extra excitement to be outdoors.

Joe was ready to move the grill into the best place for cooking without wind interruption. Three of us easily moved it into position. It looked brand new with wheels for easy mobility. The firefighters kept everything in excellent condition, and the grill was no exception. It started immediately, and smoke began to rise. Joe had plenty of help, so I went upstairs to check on the oven and appliances in the kitchen and figure out what was cooking.

As I walked the steep flight of steps, I reached the top and turned the corner and found several people upstairs visiting. I received several hugs, which made it feel more like a family reunion and less like a second visit to a community in New Jersey.

I visited with everyone upstairs, and they all volunteered to help in any way for the meal. I checked in the kitchen where a couple of people were cooking potatoes. I went back down to the parking lot, which was now full of people with kids running around laughing and yelling with faces painted. Footballs and Frisbees were being thrown, and smoke was in the air. Meat was cooking, and it seemed like everyone was really enjoying the day.

Frank and me.

After everyone had a chance to eat, Frank came up and grabbed me and asked if we could help move his dad's (Frank J's) boat, which had been pushed into a neighbor's yard by the turbulent wind and water from Superstorm Sandy. Ryan and several others came along. We went a few blocks away and were able to easily retrieve the boat and park it in Frank's driveway, where it belonged. We returned to the firehouse and fun as the sun was starting to sink in the western sky.

MORE OF SUSAN'S STRANGE TEXT

My phone rang again. I know who it is, and I am ready. It was Susan and she said, "Did you read the text?" I said, "Yes, but I don't understand how to be a tree? I don't understand why this seems to be so important to you." Her reply was, "Then read it again." Then she immediately ended the call with no explanation. Ryan was standing nearby and said, "Was that your wife?" I said, "Yes. UNBELIEVABLE! She has hung up on me three times today."

The first responders' recognition meal was a total success. The families all had a great time. The cleanup was easy with all of the volunteers pitching in. Finally, we loaded our supplies and headed to Roy and Charlotte's home to begin getting ready for our dinner, which would include ten to twelve people. Lisa had coordinated with Charlotte to take the leftovers from Sunday afternoon's meal. There was ample food, and nobody would leave hungry.

After we arrived, we all agreed to meet back at Charlotte's house around 6:30 p.m. for dinner. Blaine and Jonathan went to Joe and Lisa's to freshen up. I stayed and visited with Ryan, Roy, and Charlotte. There was still quite a bit of work left in the basement and Roy and Ryan went back to work, but Charlotte insisted that I sit down and relax. She later took me to the wall near the dining room where many family pictures were hung. She spoke warmly about the history of Little Ferry, her family, and her Italian heritage as well as Roy's family and his Norwegian/Swedish heritage.

Charlotte explained that Little Ferry was named after a rope-drawn ferry that crossed the Hackensack River from the mid-1650s to the early 1800s. The area has a lot of clay in the soil, and several brickyards sprung up early in the town's history. One of them was started by the Mehrhof brothers, and by 1882, it was the second largest brickyard in the country, producing more than 2,200,000 bricks a year.

Charlotte's grandfather, Anthony Bassano, came to Little Ferry when he was fifteen years old along with his brother, who was sixteen. Her grandfather grew up there and became the foreman at the brickyard, which was down the street from where they lived now.

In 1919, her grandfather bought the current home on Mehrhof and moved in with their six children, the youngest of which was Charlotte's father, Tom Bassano. Two more children were later born in the house.

From working at the brickyard, Anthony could bring home as many bricks as he wanted, so he used them to build the building that Ryan now lives in. Originally, it was a store that was supposed to be used for selling vegetables from the garden that was next to the driveway. That didn't last long because Charlotte's grandmother gave the food away and fed everyone in town.

Growing up in Little Ferry, Tom's passion was baseball. His skill as a catcher did not go unnoticed and he was drafted by the Cleveland Indians in 1935. However, he turned down the offer because Charlotte's mother was about to have her first child.

Tom's love of baseball led him to start organizing youth programs in town, which is why the ball field and club house are named after him. He also served on the Board of Education and as a city councilman—always doing something to serve the people of Little Ferry.

Tom worked in the printing business and, along with his two sons, started a print shop in the basement in the early 1960s. They hand set type and printed one business card at a time. He worked into the night, often after attending a baseball event or civic meeting. The business did well, so he built the garage to accommodate the growing demand.

After Charlotte told me all of this, I was awestruck. Her family had been serving the people of Little Ferry for generations. And the spot where her grandmother had given away vegetables to feed her neighbors is the same location where we had been standing for the past several days passing out food and hugs. Wow.

The rest of the evening, which included a wonderful meal and fellowship, was enjoyed by Charlotte's family, Joe and Lisa, Blaine, Jonathan, and me. Barely two weeks prior, pre-Sandy, nobody in the room (except Charlotte's immediate family) really knew each other at all. Now we were all sitting in a home bonded by love of serving others, which made the incredible amount of work worth the effort. It felt like the example of the way families should feel.

We all had more stories to share from the many people we had talked with that afternoon. Since the first responders are in the business of saving lives, they knew and shared many stories of those who had been touched by tragedy. Sandy was a grizzly force that had changed everything.

The evening ended fairly early because several in the room were returning to work. Blaine, Jonathan, and I were staying at Joe and Lisa's home, so everyone agreed to meet the next night at Joe and Lisa's for a meal since Charlotte had graciously welcomed the unexpected crowds of people for days. And she needed to return to her job the following day too. We all hugged and said good night and found our beds for much-needed rest.

As I lay in bed, I looked at my phone and again studied the text that Susan had sent. I felt informed about the message at that point. I felt prepared to discuss the text if necessary. I called to give her an update, and she sounded like a different person. We only spoke briefly about the text. I was left with the impression that she didn't even realize that she had hung up on me three times that day. Maybe we would discuss it when I got back.

The next morning, everyone awoke to the familiar scent of baked goods and breakfast in Lisa's kitchen. Coffee was brewing early, and it was the same kind she had served so many times before. Another beautiful morning, brisk temperatures, and an abundance of sunshine were on tap.

Ryan and Roy knocked on the door and joined us for a short time. Ryan had heard that the dance studio in Little Ferry was badly damaged in the storm, so volunteers were needed to assist in moving props and items to other locations. The floor was all wood and had been ruined and would need to be replaced. But the items in the studio had to be cleared out first.

Blaine worked to remove props and other items from the dance studio. Wooden floors had been ruined by the water and had to be replaced.

Blaine decided to volunteer for that project, and Jonathan decided that he was going to stay and work with Roy for the day. The damage was still so extensive that it would keep them very busy. Jonathan would see first-hand how quickly life can change. He and Roy had already grown so close that Jonathan began calling him "Uncle Roy." The sentiment seemed to touch Roy's heart. On a call from Jonathan to his mother, Roy asked to speak with her just to tell her "what a great kid Jonathan is." Blaine and Shannon also have three great daughters.

Blaine, Jonathan, and I got in the truck and headed for the dance studio around mid-morning. We found someone in the basement of the studio working on the heating and air conditioning unit. He had replaced every piece of original equipment that resulted in a very expensive repair bill. Blaine found plenty to do, so he was all set to work there, and I agreed to drop Jonathan off at Uncle Roy's. I stayed with him for a while to see what was going on.

Charlotte was busy trying to get out the door to get to work at her office—it was her first day back since the storm. She told me that Roy had a note pinned to the bulletin board in the kitchen from someone I might want to contact. The note had the name Mary Ann and a phone number written on it.

On the previous Wednesday, Mary Ann had walked several blocks from her home on Washington Street to find Roy and Charlotte's house. She had heard from some of her friends that clothing and other household items were available for free. So many items had been dropped off that we had to create a separate area just for the donations. It must have looked like a division of the Salvation Army and caused several cars to stop by and check out what we had.

When Mary Ann arrived, she went through a pile of clothes and discovered a space heater that she badly needed. After finding it, she talked with Roy, and he suggested that she take the heater home. They exchanged phone numbers, and she returned to her home.

I called the number on the note, and she answered right away. I told her that I was a friend of Roy's and was volunteering to take her to the post office, which was welcome news to her. She explained that her car had been flooded by the storm surge, and she had no transportation. We agreed that I would be going over to pick her up around 10:30 a.m. and would take her wherever she needed to go. She said that her home was easy to find, and she would be standing out front.

MEETING MARY ANN

When I arrived, she was friendly and so grateful that I had come to pick her up. Her post office box was located in Palisades Park, which was about three miles away but took about fifteen minutes to get to. The first words out of her mouth were, "I know this is a 'God thing' and the answer to my prayers that you showed up." She spoke about her own personal life history. She was of Armenian descent and had been adopted as a child. Her adoptive father had been a medical doctor, and he died early in Mary Ann's life. Her mother was left alone to raise her, which had been a challenge.

She had worked at the same job for most of her life. She was now sixty-six and had been renting the same apartment for thirty years. It was difficult for her to talk with me about herself and give accurate directions at the same time. As she talked, we took a couple of wrong turns, but it didn't matter because I was listening and taking her where she needed to go.

She said that a miracle happened to her on Sunday, and she wondered if I would like to hear it. (My immediate reaction to her statement was the "sense" that something incredible was about to happen again.) I asked her to share it. She said, "The Catholic Church near my home was giving away canned goods, including vegetables and soups, to the storm victims in need, so I decided to go and see if I could get some food." She said she went to the family center where there were sofas and chairs available, so she sat in the middle of the room and waited while church volunteers brought the items out. There were several other people in the room being waited on as well.

She said, "A beautiful young woman entered the family center. She captivated my attention immediately and seemed to be smiling constantly and gazed at me from the moment that she entered the room. She moved with poise and carried herself angelically. She made her way directly to where I was sitting. She introduced herself as a student from Oral Roberts University, and her job was to interview victims of the storm and offer emotional assistance for their tragedy.

"She offered me a booklet that described many stories regarding weather-related tragedies entitled, 'Why Me?'" Mary Ann asked, "Would you like to see the booklet now? I have it with me." Since I was driving, I said, "Thanks, but I will look at it later."

I then got the feeling that I needed to give her my undivided attention, so I pulled over. I looked at Mary Ann and waited on the rest of the story. She continued, "This woman then put her hand on my shoulder and asked if she could pray for me. I said, 'Of course.' And after the prayer, she looked at me and said, 'I have a message for you. I want you to go home and get your Bible out. I want you to turn to Psalm 1:1 and keep reading until you get tired, and then get some rest.'" I felt the familiar surge of the same supernatural energy evocative of my entire, previous weekend. I physically could not move, or say anything, for at least a minute or two. This was the same thing that Pastor Jeff had said on the previous Saturday evening when I was so distraught. Why was Mary Ann repeating a reference to the same scripture? What could it mean?

I was able to collect myself and take Mary Ann to the post office and then drop her off at a nearby grocery store. I needed a break, so I found a parking spot and sat in a total daze and stared out the window motionless. I was stunned with excitement and, paradoxically, was trying to act as though the experience never happened. I wanted to save it for a later time but be certain that I was not in a dream.

I sat for twenty minutes or so and decided to go into the store to tell Mary Ann to take her time. She was already in the checkout line, so I got the truck and met her at the front door. We visited for another thirty minutes on the way back to her home. We exchanged phone numbers, and I promised to stay in touch by phone.

I went back to Joe and Lisa's home to check in and decompress. I spoke with Blaine, and we decided to leave early on Wednesday to return to Indiana. Joe had spoken with Charlotte, and they were planning the meals for Monday and Tuesday nights. Joe's family was originally from Sicily, and he loved to cook Italian food. His special talent was making homemade olives, which took months to age to achieve the perfect flavor. It was decided that Monday's Italian meal would be at Joe and Lisa's home; and Tuesday's Italian meal would be at Roy and Charlotte's house.

Monday evening was fun, and we all roared in laughter and fellowship. Charlotte finally got to relax in someone else's home. Ryan was making fun of the way I talked again, and Jonathan shared funny stories about "Uncle Roy." The evening was amazing and filled with love, and we felt like one big family.

Tuesday morning was a repeat of Monday with work activities at the same places. I stayed with Joe and Lisa and helped them with some of their insurance needs. After lunch, Joe and I decided to get some other supplies at the store. The thought of returning home was easier this time since Blaine and Jonathan would be with me and helping me stay awake. There really was a big part of me that did not want to leave. Susan reminded me that I was needed, and she was looking forward to me coming home.

Tuesday's meal was spectacular. Joe and Charlotte had planned for the right food for the right crowd. Lisa outdid herself with her confectionary contributions. Roy got in the act with his famous potato pancakes as an appetizer. Charlotte wanted to invite everyone who had worked so hard to help us provide food, hugs, and encouragement to the more than 1,700 people we had encountered over the five or six days of cooking and serving. We had a great evening, and the dining room was filled with guests, love, and laughter.

As the evening continued, we heard stories that had not been told before. Each of us felt that we had been blessed to work together to touch so many lives through the Spirit of love.

We all said our goodnights and goodbyes as we departed down Mehrhof for the last night and walked to Joe and Lisa's home. The level of exhaustion was written on each person's face. I continued to have mixed feelings about leaving, but I knew that I was needed at home. The night ended early for Blaine, Jonathan, and me as we anticipated another 900 miles back to Indiana.

THE LONG ROAD HOME

The next morning came quickly and the house was filled with the familiar smell of Lisa's fantastic coffee, sweet rolls, and other breakfast items she had made for us to enjoy as we walked out the door. We loaded up quickly, said our goodbyes, and down Mehrhof we went.

THE RETURN TRIP

Jonathan was eager to try Lisa's breakfast casserole before we started the trip home.

Our return trip was uneventful, safe, and exhausting. Blaine and I shared equal time behind the wheel. Jonathan slept more on the return trip and more than I had noticed at any other time. We had all experienced things that we wanted to share as we drove home.

I dropped Blaine and Jonathan off at their home around 10:00 that night. Shannon, Mallory, and Elizabeth were up and waiting on our arrival. They had made chocolate chip cookies, which were fantastic, but I took mine to go. I struggled to stay awake for the remaining thirty-minute drive to get home. As I turned in the driveway, I was so excited about getting in my own bed and not in my own sleeping bag. I was greeted by barking angels, Alfie and Sophie, who seemed elated to see me. Susan was right behind the angels and very happy that we had all returned safely.

The next morning came early for both of us. Susan hit the shower, and I hit the coffee maker about 5:00 a.m. I was anxious to check my email and get caught up on so much that I had missed out on. That lasted about five minutes and I gave up. All I could process was the incredible life changing two weeks I had just spent in New Jersey. I was planning on accomplishing so many things that day but couldn't stop staring out the kitchen window.

Susan came down and we got caught up on some issues that needed to be done around the house and outside. We talked very little because she needed to get to the office. She knew where I was and knew this would take a while to understand for both of us. The reality was that neither of us was in a comfort zone and that might never change.

After she left, I went back into the kitchen and found myself staring out the window again. In an effort to break my inactivity, I went outside and took a walk in the woods as I had done after my previous return trip. Early November is a great time to enjoy the fragrances of Southern Indiana.

It seemed like every step was a struggle to let go of all that was consuming me. When I returned to the house, I went back into the kitchen and continued to stare outside for a long time. I could not get the trip and the people off my mind. I tried to meditate in prayer to find out what and why these things had happened and interpreted HIS answer to be, "KEEP SEARCHING, KEEP SEEKING, KEEP STILL, AND KNOW THAT I AM GOD."

When Susan returned home from work, I told her I had been dealing with God's prompting to call Pastor Jeff and Julie to find out if we could come up and share the New Jersey stories at his church. I told her that I knew this was an "off the wall" idea but that I felt led to call. She agreed and we immediately called Jeff.

He and Julie were excited about the idea of us coming up, and they also wanted us to spend the night with them on Saturday night. That would keep us from getting up at 1:30 a.m. for a four-hour drive. As soon as we ended the call, I was thinking about what I had just done. I completely interrupted the work and efforts that Pastor Jeff had just completed for his upcoming Sunday church service.

The next thing that Susan encouraged me to do was to develop a fifteen- to twenty-minute talk. Wow, twenty minutes to explain this amazing story. I knew that was easier said than done. We only had one more night to prepare for the talk and the trip.

We sat in the kitchen and started to discuss everything that had occurred. We were trying to sort out the stories and figure out which ones to talk about and what to say about them. All the people, all the events, the physical sensation of spinning—which seemed to be how I perceived that something "supernatural" from God was about to happen . . . how do we make sense of it and put it in a format that is meaningful to someone else?

As we were jotting down notes and developing an outline, we discussed the Psalms story and the strange coincidence of both Pastor Jeff and Mary Ann making a reference to reading the first book of Psalms. Susan asked me if I had ever read it, as Pastor Jeff had suggested, which of course I hadn't. She said, "Well maybe we should just see what it says."

She was sitting at her computer so she looked up Psalm 1 (NIV) and started reading it out loud: "1 Blessed is the one who does not walk in step with the wicked or stand in the way that sinners take or sit in the company of mockers, 2 but whose delight is in the law of the LORD, and who meditates on his law day and night. 3 That person is like a tree planted by streams of water, which yields its fruit in season and whose leaf does not wither— whatever they do prospers."

We looked at each other in stunned silence. Her seemingly strange text to me while I was in Little Ferry; the uncharacteristic behavior of calling me three times to ask me if I had read and understood the text; the more incredible response of hanging up the phone three times in a row when I said no; encouraging me to "be like a tree" all now made sense. After all, this was the woman who affirmed: "Then I suggest you get your bags packed." The words that most husbands would not want to hear were my ticket to the center of the Vortex.

All either of us could say was, "UNBELIEVABLE!"

On Saturday, we continued to fine tune the talk and selected some pictures to go with it. We got ready and made the trip with no problems, arriving at Pastor Jeff and Julie's home late in the evening. Two of the kids were away at school, and the other two were at home that night. We were glad to be there and felt welcomed by everyone. We hadn't seen the kids for a while, and they had really grown and didn't seem so much like "kids" anymore.

The next morning came early and we headed out for church. As Pastor Jeff introduced me, I was feeling a lot of anxiety and emotion and prayed for a smooth delivery. I walked up to the lectern, notes in hand, and said how much I appreciated being there, and that was the end of my prepared remarks. I did not follow one thing on the paper. I spoke from my heart and delivered a testimony, amid sweat and tears, that I barely remember. Pastor Jeff skillfully wove his message into what I had said to create a moving and powerful conclusion to the service. The next two services were similar to the first but Susan told me afterwards that I hadn't said the same thing twice in any of the services.

At the end of each service, we shook hands and chatted with people as they were leaving. Several people said, "You should write a book." Surprisingly, three of the couples who made the suggestion were from Bergen County and had grown up within a few miles of Little Ferry.

We had lunch with Jeff, Julie, and the kids, which was fun, but we felt rushed to get home to take care of the dogs. We said our goodbyes and headed for home. I asked Susan to drive to give me a chance to relax after speaking at the three services. It felt great to have the services behind me, but more questions seemed to emerge. I tried to make sense of the purpose of being led to Jeff's church in the first place.

The following weeks continued to deflate my excitement as a new reality was starting to settle in—the reality of trying to return to a "normal" life. Nothing was the same, and I felt inspired to keep telling the story, but why? I wondered if I should try to write a book, but what would I say? I didn't think that my life was any kind of example that would qualify me to write a book. As I faced these issues, I had more questions than answers, and I felt lost.

It seemed as though I was spinning through space passing billboards along the way that read:

The Party Is Over

What Was Wrong with the Comfort Zone?

Public Speaking Is Not for You

You Are Not a Writer—Forget a Book

Why Would You Want to Speak in a Church?
Nobody Would Listen to You.

These negative messages sounded very similar to those I had heard when I started on my first trip to the East Coast.

I thought it was important to maintain contact with a few friends who could help me to discern the right steps to move forward. Those conversations were a mixture of encouragement and a kick in the gut. One friend suggested that I write excerpts from the "trip" for a magazine. Another friend asked, "Why would you write a book?" Biting my lip (nearly in half), I left those meetings deflated and discouraged—but determined to find the answer.

It seemed that I was being tempted to the old practice of seeking approval of others instead of listening to what I heard inside my heart. This type of behavior was something I intended to change—that day. One thing wasn't changing—I could not stop thinking about what had happened. I was in a constant state of confusion about what to do. I couldn't find the answers by talking to friends; prayer was yielding no answers; and studying scriptures was only providing temporary relief.

I had dealt with all of these issues, and yet something was waking me up each night with thoughts about the book. The negative thoughts about writing seemed to fade away as I began putting the experiences down on paper. As I typed, I felt that more about the experience was being revealed to me. Because of the extraordinary events on Saturday, my main focus had been on the chapter, "Miracles on Mehrhof." I relived every moment in the driveway as though I was watching a movie with one question: Why did YOU do that to me? I felt like the answer was, "KEEP TYPING AND I WILL SHOW YOU WHEN I AM READY."

I continued to type, and I continued to listen. At a new level I understood that as we initially watched the storm on television, empathy for the victims became impressions in the heart. Impressions in the heart became a passion to respond. The response became a physical mission, and the physical mission became a spiritual journey. There were times that I felt as if the words were lifting off the page and speaking into my face. Understanding seemed to be slowly moving toward discernment. Susan and I knew it was in the right direction.

We also checked on our friends in New Jersey to see how they were doing. For some, day-to-day life was getting back to normal, but nearly everyone was dealing with mountains of paperwork in the hope of getting financial assistance for their losses.

While Susan and I were still trying to understand the meaning of the New Jersey trip, an EF5 tornado hit Moore, Oklahoma. The devastation was incredible with wind gusts over 210 miles per hour. Susan heard about the storm and called to say that she thought that I was supposed to respond, but only if someone could go with me. She encouraged me to ask Eddie, a friend from Methodist Temple. We didn't think Eddie would be able to go because of his work schedule, but his name kept coming up in my mind too. I called him, and it just so happened that he was planning on taking the week off, so he might be able to go. He called back a short time later and said that the trip was on for him.

Eddie and I headed out on our 700-mile journey and planned on cooking for three days. When we arrived in the area, we met another group that was grilling food so we parked beside them every day. I cooked and Eddie handed out food on paper plates for people driving by—almost like a drive-up window. Many of the policemen got to know him as they came by on their four-wheelers. Eddie was very organized and had their plates covered in aluminum foil and ready to go. On the final day, we got rerouted to a new entrance, and there was a long line of homeowners and other service vehicles waiting to get in. When we drove up, I had doubts about whether we would get into the area until a policeman recognized Eddie and waved us through, saying, "Hey Eddie, I hope that you'll have more of your famous kielbasa sausage today." Eddie replied that he would be standing in the very same place as on previous days.

Eddie is ready to serve with hot dogs in hand.

We were grateful for the opportunity to serve and touch many lives. We returned home and laughed about some of the people we met while in Oklahoma. The experience bonded our friendship, and we occasionally mention the trip when we see each other.

PART TWO

ANATOMY OF VORTEX OF THE HOLY SPIRIT

I kept working on the book—often at 2:00 a.m. with fresh coffee and a quiet space. Susan and I continued to give many hours of thought and discussion to the narrative of the book, but we were feeling like there was much more to do. During this time, I heard the words "Holy Spirit" whispered into my consciousness almost continuously. Susan was also experiencing the same thing except that she received thoughts in her dreams, and I was being led mostly when I was typing. We tried to stay alert to any insights we might have.

We did not understand the role of the Holy Spirit in what had happened, but we began to do research about Him as though we had been diagnosed with an incurable disease and wanted to know everything about it: what the symptoms were and how it behaved once in our bodies. It felt like we were being guided in a new direction. He would repeat Himself to say, "I assembled and coordinated all the circumstances and events that happened in New Jersey, and I am still coordinating for both of you." So there was no question that "Holy Spirit" would be in the title of the book, but we still didn't know how.

One afternoon, Susan and I were walking at the county fairgrounds near our house. We were taking the loop that we usually walked and were climbing the tallest hill on the route. We were talking about the trip to the East Coast, which was consuming nearly every minute of our conversation time.

As we continued walking toward the top of the hill, we were discussing a weather alert that I had heard about earlier in the day. A storm within 300 miles of our location had uprooted many trees and caused significant damage. Strangely, the one thing that I remembered from the news was that the "vortex" of the storm was nearly one mile in diameter. Susan said, "Vortex . . . that's an intriguing word."

We both stopped walking and looked at each other and knew that we had just been given the title of this book: "Vortex of the Holy Spirit!" We were elated about how and what had just taken place. This breakthrough also reinforced the feeling that the Holy Spirit was now speaking to us as a team. We finished our walk, and the pace increased significantly as we finished the final lap.

In the following weeks, I could not get the vortex concept out of my mind. I came home and turned on the television, and the symbol of our cable company looked exactly like a vortex. I remember leaving one morning for an early meeting, and light snow had fallen on my hood during the night. As I increased speed on the driveway, the snow spiraled upward in the shape of a vortex on both sides of the hood. I went to Dallas to visit my son, and as the plane lifted off the runway, I saw two perfectly spiraled vortices spinning from either wing. I came home, and we ate dinner using the plates that we rarely used. In the center of the plate was a vortex. A light had burned out above the table, and as I looked up, I noticed that the fixture attached was a vortex turned upside down. I cleaned up the dishes and had water in the sink. When I released the drain, another vortex appeared in the water. It seemed as though I was obsessing, but I believed that I was getting help with the imagery.

Our next challenge was to define what "Vortex of the Holy Spirit" meant to us, what purpose it served, and how to explain it to someone else. We talked about it, prayed about it, and researched multiple resources. We started with the word "vortex." We found the first definition below in the Encarta Dictionary, English, North America version, and the second one at Dictionary.com, in the British Dictionary definition area.

Vortex \vawr-teks\ noun

1. A whirling mass of wind, water or air that draws everything near it toward its center

2. Any activity, situation, or way of life regarded as irresistibly engulfing

"Vortex" evolved to represent the world in which we all live. We fill every minute of the day with schedules of life's activities: going to work, going to school, keeping doctor appointments, making trips to the grocery, picking the kids up, getting the car repaired, meeting a friend for lunch, watching the news on television, etc. We further complicate our lives, now, with the convenience of the cell phone—not only as a phone, but also as a handheld computer that allows us to check our email, exchange text messages, follow Twitter, post on Facebook, play games, research any topic, track our health, and much more. It seems like the only free time we do have, we lose to the cell phone.

The seasons of life change, but our schedules stay busy for children, adults, parents, and grandparents. We all spin around this circle of life and try to manage everything; some of us seek the help of the Holy Spirit, and many do not.

CALLING OUT TO GOD IN THE VORTEX

When my daughter, Andrea, was born, she had become entangled with the umbilical cord during the birthing process. By the time she "entered" the room, the cord had coiled around her neck restricting the blood flow and causing her to be as blue as a crayon. Andrea was not responsive or breathing on her own, so the doctor quickly took her to a table designed for treating babies. I followed every step and stayed within inches of everything he was doing to my daughter!

For me, the room was "spinning like a vortex" and I was to be drawn to the center, imploring God to spare this precious little life. The nurse called out every fifteen seconds, but Andrea was not responding, and tension permeated the room. I suddenly heard a steady, rhythmic, thumping noise, which I discovered was the pounding of my own heart.

The doctor's focus intensified as his efforts to resuscitate Andrea continued. His final decision was to inject her with epinephrine; a neurotransmitter used in emergency situations to stimulate the body's fight-or-flight response. It was like receiving a huge dose of adrenaline. The moment it hit her bloodstream, she opened her eyes and screamed for all to hear! I noticed that both of her irises and whites of her eyes were blue; but she was now conscious and moving on her own. Now twenty-eight years later, Andrea serves babies and families as a neonatal intensive care unit (NICU) nurse.

The miracle of Andrea's birth metaphorically illustrates where we all can find ourselves in the vortex as adults. Andrea: she had become entangled with the umbilical cord as she made her way through the vortex of the birth process. Us: we become entangled as we make our way through the vortex of life and drift away from the Holy Spirit. Andrea: the doctor's focus intensified as efforts were failing. Us: the Holy Spirit can turn up His volume if we are not responding to His desire to reach us. Andrea: His final decision was to inject her with epinephrine. Us: the Holy Spirit can use many strategies to get our attention. He will decide when the final decision is.

This reminds us that everything in our world can change in a heartbeat. A routine doctor's appointment can bring a serious diagnosis; a change at work can result in the loss of a job; an accident can lead to unexpected problems; or family issues can cause sadness or disappointment. We toil and grieve and spin in the vortex to find the answer to:

1. WHO is going to help me with this?
2. WHAT can my faith do for me now?
3. WHEN will this pain be over?
4. WHERE will this path take me?

WHEN we are so stunned, we may instinctively go to the center of the vortex but not realize how we got there, WHO is there with us, WHAT faith can do to change the circumstances, and WHERE we go from here.

A MERRY-GO-ROUND MODEL OF THE VORTEX

I grew up in a small town called Fort Branch, which is about fifteen miles north of Evansville. The community park had a playground that I visited many times as a kid. It had the typical swing sets, teeter-totters, and slides that most playgrounds have. The ride I spent most of my time on was the merry-go-round. This was not the kind of merry-go-round one sees at amusement parks with colorful horses and carrousel music. This ride had a wooden platform that was about a foot off the ground and was nine or ten feet in diameter.

The platform was divided into six equal sections. Each section was separated by safety bars connected to a sturdy center post from which the ride was suspended. If I was alone, I would start running around the outside and push the bars to build up speed. When the ride was rotating fast enough, I jumped on! While sitting near the edge, the force pushing outward was powerful, and hanging on required constant effort. Spinning around with my hair blowing in the wind was fun and evoked a sense of freedom—but holding on was a must.

The best part of the ride was moving into the center. As soon as I reached the center, my entire experience changed. The horizontal force that had previously pushed me toward the outside was replaced by a vertical force that kept me grounded, and there was a completely different sensation. The center felt safe and was "where the resistance stopped." Once there, it was easy to stay seated and hold on. After building confidence, I could even stand up as the ride continued to spin. While standing in the center, all the force that had previously pushed me to the outside was gone. I could relax, catch my breath, and get ready to do it all again.

The calm at the center of a merry-go-round is a metaphor for the calm we find when our lives are centered on God.

The experiences on the merry-go-round represent our lives as adults and the difference we feel between being caught up in the activities of our lives—as in the outer portion of a vortex—and being centered on God and spiritual renewal—as in the inner portion of the vortex.

The benefit of being grounded in the center of the vortex is that it helps us stay focused on God and listen for His voice in our hearts. In John 10:27 (NIV), Jesus says, "My sheep listen to my voice; I know them, and they follow me." If our attention is diverted, we drift away from the center and out into the vortex on our own. God's voice and messaging never stop, but our attention does. Like the merry-go-round, moving outward in the vortex increases the speed at which we spin. As the spin increases, we become consumed with "our world" which impedes listening. The moment we stop listening is the moment that deception begins to creep into our lives.

Deception occurs when we believe that what we hear is from the Holy Spirit but it turns out to be another influence. We hear *this* influence in our heads and it cheers us on: "way to go; look at you; you are awesome; you don't need any help." We get caught up in this process, which grows and feeds our pride. Notice the "I" in the middle of the word "pride," which is a reminder for "it's all about me." This pattern grows until we fall, and back to the center of the vortex to the Holy Spirit we go.

The following table helps explain the relevance of this model:

MERRY-GO-ROUND EXPERIENCE	METAPHOR FOR EVERYDAY LIFE IN THE VORTEX	GUIDANCE FROM SCRIPTURE
"The force pushing outward was powerful"	The further from the center we are, the more resistance we feel.	We must pay the most careful attention, therefore, to what we have heard, so that we do not drift away. (Heb. 2:1 NIV)
"Hanging on required constant effort"	Life is hectic, and it takes a lot of energy to keep going.	Consider it pure joy, my brothers and sisters, whenever you face trials of many kinds, because you know that the testing of your faith produces perseverance. (James 1:2–3 NIV
"The best part of the ride was moving to the center"	The Holy Spirit draws us to the center.	And I, when I am lifted up from the earth, will draw all people to myself. (John 12:32 NIV)

MERRY-GO-ROUND EXPERIENCE	METAPHOR FOR EVERYDAY LIFE IN THE VORTEX	GUIDANCE FROM SCRIPTURE
"Where the resistance stops"	We find answers in the center of the vortex, grounded in the Holy Spirit.	Be still, and know that I am God. (Ps. 46:10 NIV)
"You could relax, catch your breath, and get ready to do it all again"	The Holy Spirit educates us, empowers us, and enables us to live our lives and face our challenges.	Come to me, all you who are weary and burdened, and I will give you rest. Take my yoke upon you and learn from me, for I am gentle and humble in heart, and you will find rest for your souls. (Matt. 11:28–29 NIV)

WHO IS THE HOLY SPIRIT ANYWAY?

The phrase, "In the name of the Father, and of the Son, and of the Holy Ghost" pretty much summed up my understanding of the Holy Spirit. The phrase was often said at the end of a prayer, and I didn't think too much more about it. Of course, I knew that the Godhead was referred to as three persons, or the Trinity that includes God, Jesus, and the Holy Spirit—but that was about the extent of it.

I was most familiar with father-son part of the relationship. However, the Holy Spirit seemed mysterious, and my awareness of His part of the Trinity was limited. Maybe I just hadn't been listening . . .

After the events following Superstorm Sandy, Susan and I began a search to find out more about the Holy Spirit. Being aware that we needed any information to be based in scripture, we rolled up our sleeves and dived into the Bible and other resources in order to learn what we could.

What we soon realized is that we didn't really know much about the third person of the Trinity, the Holy Spirit. (For comparison: A six cylinder engine with one third fewer cylinders would presume the engine to be running on four cylinders instead of six. The full power is reduced thirty-three-and-a-third percent for the purpose of which it was intended.)

We started with a basic definition of the word "spirit" in both Hebrew (the original language of the Old Testament) and Greek (the original language of the New Testament). In Hebrew, "spirit" is translated as "Ruach," meaning wind, breath, or spirit. "Spirit" is translated from Greek as "Pneuma," meaning a current of air, breath, breeze, or spirit. (The English word "pneumatic" is derived from it.) It is interesting to note that these two definitions include air or wind, and the definition of "vortex" is a whirling mass of air that draws everything near it toward its center.

Then we turned to the Holy Spirit as part of the Trinity. We had often seen the diagram below, which we thought was a simple, yet effective, way to describe this complex, and often confusing, relationship.

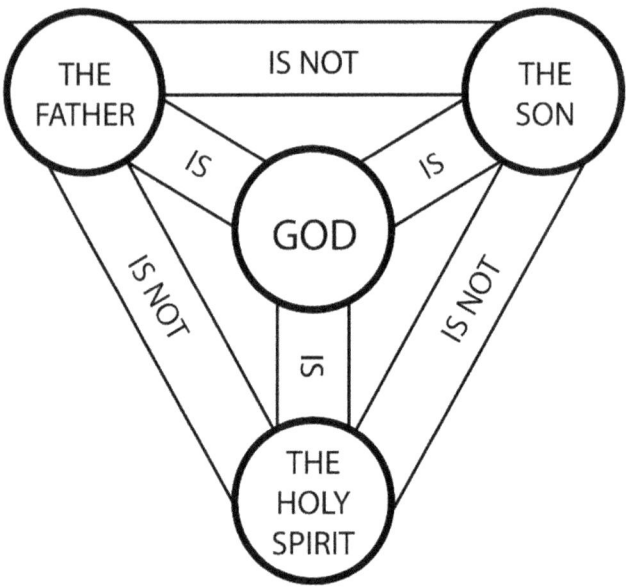

After looking into it, it turns out that the diagram and its related creed are quite old. The creed is attributed to Athanasius, a fourth century bishop of Alexandria who was the strongest defender of the doctrines of the Trinity and the divinity of Christ at the time. We thought the language of the creed was among the most illuminating explanations we could find:

EXCERPTS FROM THE ATHANASIAN CREED

For there is one Person of the Father, another of the Son, and another of the Holy Spirit. But the godhead of the Father, of the Son, and of the Holy Spirit, is all one, the glory equal, the majesty co-eternal.

The Father eternal, the Son eternal, and the Holy Spirit eternal. And yet they are not three eternals, but one Eternal.

So the Father is God, the Son is God, and the Holy Spirit is God. And yet they are not three gods, but one God.

So likewise the Father is Lord, the Son Lord, and the Holy Spirit Lord. And yet not three lords, but one Lord.

So there is one Father, not three fathers; one Son, not three sons; one Holy Spirit, not three holy spirits.

And in the Trinity none is before or after another; none is greater or less than another, but all three Persons are co-eternal together and co-equal. So that in all things, as is aforesaid, the Unity in Trinity and the Trinity in Unity is to be worshipped.

We began searching and cataloguing Scripture about the Holy Spirit. Among the hundreds of times He is mentioned throughout the Bible, this instance stood out—I couldn't get my mind off of it. While we don't understand the full meaning and impact of these verses from Matthew, we thought anything this important warranted our full attention.

> *And so I tell you, every kind of sin and slander can be forgiven, but blasphemy against the **Spirit** will not be forgiven. Anyone who speaks a word against the Son of Man will be forgiven, but anyone who speaks against the **Holy Spirit** will not be forgiven, either in this age or in the age to come.* (Matt. 12:31-32 NIV, emphasis added)

We also learned about the role of the Holy Spirit in many of the most significant events in the history of the earth. The following information is not intended to be an exhaustive study of the Holy Spirit, but these examples were meaningful to us as a way to explore the eternal nature of the Holy Spirit.

THE HOLY SPIRIT THROUGHOUT HISTORY

In the beginning:

> *In the beginning God created the heaven and the earth. And the earth was without form, and void; and darkness was upon the face of the deep. And the **Spirit of God** moved upon the face of the waters.* (Gen. 1:1–2 KJV, emphasis added)

From water in the womb to water in the Jordan: John the Baptist and Jesus. The announcement of the birth of John the Baptist:

> *But the angel said to him: "Do not be afraid, Zechariah; your prayer has been heard. Your wife Elizabeth will bear you a son, and you are to call him John. He will be a joy and delight to you, and many will rejoice because of his birth, for he will be great in the sight of the Lord. He is never to take wine or other fermented drink, and he will be filled with the **Holy Spirit** even before he is born.* (Luke 1:13–15 NIV, emphasis added)

The announcement of the birth of Jesus:

> *But the angel said to her, "Do not be afraid, Mary; you have found favor with God. You will conceive and give birth to a son, and you are to call him Jesus. He will be great and will be called the Son of the Most High.* (Luke 1:30–32 NIV)

> *"How will this be," Mary asked the angel, "since I am a virgin?" The angel answered, "The **Holy Spirit** will come on you, and the power of the Most High will overshadow you. So the holy one to be born will be called the Son of God. Even*

> *Elizabeth your relative is going to have a child in her old age, and she who was said to be unable to conceive is in her sixth month. For no word from God will ever fail." "I am the Lord's servant," Mary answered. "May your word to me be fulfilled." Then the angel left her.* (Luke 1:34–38 NIV, emphasis added)

Mary visits Elizabeth:

> *At that time Mary got ready and hurried to a town in the hill country of Judea, where she entered Zechariah's home and greeted Elizabeth. When Elizabeth heard Mary's greeting, the baby leaped in her womb, and Elizabeth was filled with the **Holy Spirit**. In a loud voice she exclaimed: "Blessed are you among women, and blessed is the child you will bear! But why am I so favored, that the mother of my Lord should come to me? As soon as the sound of your greeting reached my ears, the baby in my womb leaped for joy. Blessed is she who has believed that the Lord would fulfill his promises to her!"* (Luke 1:39–44 NIV, emphasis added)

Baptism of Jesus by John the Baptist:

> *When all the people were being baptized, Jesus was baptized too. And as he was praying, heaven was opened and the **Holy Spirit** descended on him in bodily form like a dove. And a voice came from heaven: "You are my Son, whom I love; with you I am well pleased."* (Luke 3:21–22 NIV, emphasis added)

Jesus promises the Holy Spirit:

> *"If you love me, keep my commands. And I will ask the Father, and he will give you another **Counselor** to help you and be with you forever— the **Spirit** of truth.* (John 14:15–17 NIV, emphasis added)

> In the original Greek version of the New Testament, the word used to describe the Holy Spirit is "Parakletos," which means to comfort, encourage, or exhort. In addition to "Counselor," other biblical translations use similar words such as "Comforter," "Helper," and "Advocate."

> *The world cannot accept him, because it neither sees him nor knows him. But you know him, for he lives **with** you and will be **in** you. I will not leave you as orphans; I will come to you. Before long, the world will not see me anymore, but you will see me. Because I live, you also will live. On that day you will realize that I am in my Father, and you are in me, and I am in you.* (John 14:17–20 NIV, emphasis added)

> (Note the significance of **with** you and **in** you.)

Trinity at work: the Father sends the Holy Spirit in the name of Jesus Christ:

> *"All this I have spoken while still with you. But the **Counselor**, the **Holy Spirit**, whom the Father will send in my name, will teach you all things and will remind you of everything I have said to you. Peace I leave with you; my peace I give you. I do not give to you as the world gives. Do not let your hearts be troubled and do not be afraid.* (John 14:25–27 NIV, emphasis added)

Jesus must leave and send the Holy Spirit:

> *But very truly I tell you, it is for your good that I am going away. Unless I go away, the **Counselor** will not come to you; but if I go, I will send him to you. When he comes, he will prove the world to be in the wrong about sin and righteousness and judgment: about sin, because people do not believe in me; about righteousness, because I am going to the Father, where you can see me no longer; and about judgment, because the prince of this world now stands condemned.* (John 16:7–11 NIV, emphasis added)

Arrival of the Holy Spirit and establishing the Christian church:

> *When the day of Pentecost came, they were all together in one place* [120 believers]. *Suddenly a sound like the blowing of a violent wind came from heaven and filled the whole house where they were sitting. They saw what seemed to be tongues of fire that separated and came to rest on each of them. All of them were filled with the **Holy Spirit** and began to speak in other tongues* [languages] *as the **Spirit** enabled them.* (Acts 2:1–4 NIV, emphasis added) ("Pentecost," meaning fiftieth, falls on the fiftieth day after Easter.)

Life through the Spirit:

> *Therefore, there is now no condemnation for those who are in Christ Jesus, because through Christ Jesus the law of the **Spirit** who gives life has set you free from the law of sin and death. For what the law was powerless to do because it was weakened by the flesh, God did by sending his own Son in the likeness of sinful man to be a sin*

> *offering. And so he condemned sin in the flesh, in order that the righteous requirement of the law might be fully met in us, who do not live according to the flesh but according to the **Spirit**.*
>
> *Those who live according to the flesh have their minds set on what the flesh desires; but those who live in accordance with the **Spirit** have their minds set on what the **Spirit** desires. The mind governed by the flesh is death, but the mind governed by the **Spirit** is life and peace. The mind governed by the flesh is hostile to God; it does not submit to God's law, nor can it do so. Those who are in the realm of the flesh cannot please God.* (Rom. 8:1–8 NIV, emphasis added)

Holy Spirit that raised Christ lives in us:

> *And if the **Spirit** of him who raised Jesus from the dead is living in you, he who raised Christ from the dead will also give life to your mortal bodies because of his **Spirit** who lives in you.* (Rom. 8:11 NIV, emphasis added)

THE HOLY SPIRIT TODAY: FIFTY WAYS THE HOLY SPIRIT WORKS IN OUR EVERYDAY LIVES

In addition, we found the following scriptures that describe some of the many ways in which the Holy Spirit helps us throughout our lives.

1) The Spirit glorifies Jesus.

> *When the Counselor comes, whom I will send to you from the Father—the Spirit of truth who goes out from the Father—he will testify about me.* (John 15:26 NIV)

> *Therefore I want you to know that no one who is speaking by the Spirit of God says, "Jesus be cursed," and no one can say, "Jesus is Lord," except by the Holy Spirit.* (1 Cor. 12:3 NIV)

2) The Spirit is given by Jesus.

> *Again Jesus said, "Peace be with you! As the Father has sent me, I am sending you." And with that he breathed on them and said, "Receive the Holy Spirit."* (John 20:21 NIV)

3) The Spirit gives birth to our spirit.

> *Jesus answered, "Very truly I tell you, no one can enter the kingdom of God unless they are born of water and the Spirit. Flesh gives birth to flesh, but the Spirit gives birth to spirit.* (John 3:5–6 NIV)

> *I will give you a new heart and put a new spirit in you; I will remove from you your heart of stone and give you a heart of flesh. And I will put my*

Spirit in you and move you to follow my decrees and be careful to keep my laws. (Ezek. 36:26–27 NIV)

4) The Spirit seals us.

And you also were included in Christ when you heard the message of truth, the gospel of your salvation. When you believed, you were marked in him with a seal, the promised Holy Spirit, who is a deposit guaranteeing our inheritance until the redemption of those who are God's possession—to the praise of his glory. (Eph. 1:13–14 NIV)

Now it is God who makes both us and you stand firm in Christ. He anointed us, set his seal of ownership on us, and put his Spirit in our hearts as a deposit, guaranteeing what is to come. (2 Cor. 1:21–22 NIV)

5) The Spirit testifies that we are children of God.

The Spirit himself testifies with our spirit that we are God's children. (Rom. 8:16 NIV)

6) The Spirit lives in us.

And in him you too are being built together to become a dwelling in which God lives by his Spirit. (Eph. 2:22 NIV)

Don't you know that you yourselves are God's temple and that God's Spirit dwells in your midst? (1 Cor. 3:16 NIV)

7) The Spirit leads us.

> *But if you are led by the Spirit, you are not under the law.* (Gal. 5:18 NIV)

> *For those who are led by the Spirit of God are the children of God.* (Rom. 8:14 NIV)

8) The Spirit teaches us about spiritual truths.

> *This is what we speak, not in words taught us by human wisdom but in words taught by the Spirit, explaining spiritual realities with Spirit-taught words.* (1 Cor. 2:13 NIV)

9) The Spirit directs us to life in Christ.

> *You, however, are not in the realm of the flesh but are in the realm of the Spirit, if indeed the Spirit of God lives in you. And if anyone does not have the Spirit of Christ, they do not belong to Christ.* (Rom. 8:9 NIV)

10) The Spirit reveals things to come.

> *I have much more to say to you, more than you can now bear. But when he, the Spirit of truth, comes, he will guide you into all the truth. He will not speak on his own; he will speak only what he hears, and he will tell you what is yet to come. He will glorify me because it is from me that he will receive what he will make known to you. All that belongs to the Father is mine. That is why I said the Spirit will receive from me what he will make known to you.* (John 16:12–15 NIV)

> *However, as it is written: "What no eye has seen, what no ear has heard, and what no human mind has conceived"—the things God has prepared for*

those who love him—these are the things God has revealed to us by his Spirit. (1 Cor. 2:9–10 NIV)

11) The Spirit distributes gifts.

There are different kinds of gifts, but the same Spirit distributes them. There are different kinds of service, but the same Lord. There are different kinds of working, but in all of them and in everyone it is the same God at work. Now to each one the manifestation of the Spirit is given for the common good. (1 Cor. 12:4–7 NIV)

God also testified to it by signs, wonders and various miracles, and by gifts of the Holy Spirit distributed according to his will. (Heb. 2:4 NIV)

12) The Spirit bears fruit in our lives.

But the fruit of the Spirit is love, joy, peace, forbearance, kindness, goodness, faithfulness, gentleness and self-control. Against such things there is no law. (Gal. 5:22–23 NIV)

13) The Spirit emboldens us.

After they prayed, the place where they were meeting was shaken. And they were all filled with the Holy Spirit and spoke the word of God boldy. (Acts 4:31 NIV)

14) The Spirit speaks to us.

Whoever has ears, let them hear what the Spirit says to the churches. To the one who is victorious, I will give the right to eat from the tree of life, which is in the paradise of God. (Rev. 2:7 NIV)

15) The Spirit unites us.

> *Just as a body, though one, has many parts, but all its many parts form one body, so it is with Christ. For we were all baptized by one Spirit so as to form one body—whether Jews or Gentiles, slave or free—and we were all given the one Spirit to drink.* (1 Cor. 12:12–13 NIV)

> *Make every effort to keep the unity of the Spirit through the bond of peace. There is one body and one Spirit, just as you were called to one hope when you were called; one Lord, one faith, one baptism; one God and Father of all, who is over all and through all and in all.* (Eph. 4:3–6 NIV)

16) The Spirit transforms us.

> *The Spirit of the LORD will come powerfully upon you, and you will prophesy with them; and you will be changed into a different person.* (1 Sam. 10:6 NIV)

> *But we all, with open face beholding as in a glass the glory of the Lord, are changed into the same image from glory to glory, even as by the Spirit of the Lord.* (2 Cor. 3:18 KJV)

> *Now the Lord is the Spirit, and where the Spirit of the Lord is, there is freedom. And we all, who with unveiled faces contemplate the Lord's glory, are being transformed into his image with ever-increasing glory, which comes from the Lord, who is the Spirit.* (2 Cor. 3:17–18 NIV)

17) The Spirit flows within us.

> *"Let anyone who is thirsty come to me and drink. Whoever believes in me, as scripture has said, rivers of living water will flow from within them." By this he meant the Spirit, whom those who believed in him were to later receive. Up to that time the Spirit had not been given, since Jesus had not yet been glorified.* (John 7:36–39 NIV)

18) The Spirit appoints ministries.

> *Keep watch over yourselves and all the flock of which the Holy Spirit has made you overseers. Be shepherds of the church of God, which he bought with his own blood.* (Acts 20:28 NIV)

19) The Spirit anoints us.

> *As for you, the anointing you received from him remains in you, and you do not need anyone to teach you. But as his anointing teaches you about all things and as that anointing is real, not counterfeit—just as it has taught you, remain in him.* (1 John 2:27 NIV)

20) The Spirit assures God's love.

> *And hope does not put us to shame, because God's love has been poured out into our hearts through the Holy Spirit, who has been given to us.* (Rom. 5:5 NIV)

21) The Spirit intercedes for us.

> *In the same way, the Spirit helps us in our weakness. We do not know what we ought to pray for, but the Spirit himself intercedes for us*

through wordless groans. And he who searches our hearts knows the mind of the Spirit, because the Spirit intercedes for God's people in accordance with the will of God. (Rom. 8:26–27 NIV)

22) The Spirit protects us.

Take the helmet of salvation and the sword of the Spirit, which is the word of God. (Eph. 6:17 NIV)

23) The Spirit frees us from the law of sin and death.

Therefore, there is now no condemnation for those who are in Christ Jesus, because through Christ Jesus the law of the Spirit who gives life has set you free from the law of sin and death. (Rom. 8:1–2 NIV)

24) The Spirit brings prophesy, dreams, and visions.

In the last days, God says, I will pour out my Spirit on all people. Your sons and daughters will prophesy, your young men will see visions, your old men will dream dreams. (Acts 2:17 NIV)

25) The Spirit prophesies through us.

For prophecy never had its origin in the human will, but prophets, though human, spoke from God as they were carried along by the Holy Spirit. (2 Pet. 1:21 NIV)

26) The Spirit baptizes us.

For John baptized with water, but in a few days you will be baptized with the Holy Spirit. (Acts 1:5 NIV)

> *Therefore go and make disciples of all nations, baptizing them in the name of the Father and of the Son and of the Holy Spirit* (Matt. 28:19 NIV)

27) The Spirit fills us.

> *Do not get drunk on wine, which leads to debauchery. Instead be filled with the Spirit, speaking to one another in psalms, hymns, and songs from the Spirit. Sing and make music from your heart to the Lord, always giving thanks to God the Father for everything, in the name of our Lord Jesus Christ.* (Eph. 5:18–20 NIV)

> *But as for me, I am filled with power, with the Spirit of the LORD, and with justice and might* (Micah 3:8 NIV)

28) The Spirit empowers us.

> *I am going to send you what my Father has promised; but stay in the city until you have been clothed with power from on high.* (Luke 24:49 NIV)

> *But you will receive power when the Holy Spirit comes on you* (Acts 1:8 NIV)

29) The Spirit helps us remember God's teaching.

> *What you heard from me, keep as the pattern of sound teaching, with faith and love in Christ Jesus. Guard the good deposit that was entrusted to you—guard it with the help of the Holy Spirit who lives in us.* (2 Tim. 1:13–14 NIV)

30) The Spirit teaches us about the forgiveness of sin.

For by one sacrifice he has made perfect forever those who are being made holy. The Holy Spirit also testifies to us about this. First he says: "This is the covenant I will make with them after that time, says the Lord. I will put my laws in their hearts, and I will write them on their minds."

Then he adds: "Their sins and lawless acts I will remember no more." And where these have been forgiven, sacrifice for sin is no longer necessary. (Heb. 10:14–18 NIV)

31) The Spirit sanctifies us.

But we ought always to thank God for you, brothers and sisters loved by the Lord, because God chose you as firstfruits to be saved through the sanctifying work of the Spirit and through belief in the truth. (2 Thess. 2:13 NIV)

32) The Spirit strengthens us.

I pray that out of his glorious riches he may strengthen you with power through his Spirit in your inner being (Eph. 3:16 NIV)

33) The Spirit renews us.

He saved us, not because of righteous things we had done, but because of his mercy. He saved us through the washing of rebirth and renewal by the Holy Spirit (Titus 3:5 NIV)

34) The Spirit guarantees our future.

Now the one who has fashioned us for this very purpose is God, who has given us the Spirit as a deposit, guaranteeing what is to come. (2 Cor. 5:5 NIV)

35) The Spirit brings good news.

The Spirit of the Sovereign LORD is on me, because the LORD has anointed me to proclaim good news to the poor. He has sent me to bind up the brokenhearted, to proclaim freedom for the captives and release from darkness for the prisoners. (Isa. 61:1 NIV)

To comfort all who mourn, and provide for those who grieve in Zion—to bestow on them a crown of beauty instead of ashes, the oil of joy instead of mourning, and a garment of praise instead of a spirit of despair. They will be called oaks of righteousness, a planting of the LORD for the display of his splendor. (Isa. 61:3 NIV)

36) The Spirit enables hope in us.

For through the Spirit we eagerly await by faith the righteousness for which we hope. (Gal. 5:5 NIV)

37) The Spirit guides us away from sin.

So I say, walk by the Spirit, and you will not gratify the desires of the flesh. (Gal. 5:16 NIV)

38) The Spirit provides access to the Father.

He [Jesus Christ] came and preached peace to you who were far away and peace to those who were near. For through him we both have access to the Father by one Spirit. (Eph. 2:17–18 NIV)

39) The Spirit assures us that Christ abides with us.

> *The one who keeps God's commands lives in him, and he in them. And this is how we know that he lives in us: We know it by the Spirit he gave us.* (1 John 3:24 NIV)

40) The Spirit reveals God's thoughts to us.

> *For who knows a person's thoughts except their own spirit within them? In the same way no one knows the thoughts of God except the Spirit of God.* (1 Cor. 2:11 NIV)

41) The Spirit helps us pray.

> *And pray in the Spirit on all occasions with all kinds of prayers and requests. With this in mind, be alert and always keep on praying for all the Lord's people.* (Eph. 6:18 NIV)

42) The Spirit shows us what is pleasing to God.

> *For the kingdom of God is not a matter of eating and drinking, but of righteousness, peace and joy in the Holy Spirit, because anyone who serves Christ in this way is pleasing to God and receives human approval.* (Rom. 14:17–18 NIV)

43) The Spirit inspires us to speak.

> *For the Holy Spirit will teach you at that time what you should say.* (Luke 12:12 NIV)

44) The Spirit teaches us about God.

> *I keep asking that the God of our Lord Jesus Christ, the glorious Father, may give you the Spirit of wisdom and revelation, so that you may know him better.* (Eph. 1:17 NIV)

45) The Spirit bears witness about the resurrection of Jesus Christ.

> *The God of our ancestors raised Jesus from the dead* (Acts 5:30 NIV)

> *We are witnesses of these things, and so is the Holy Spirit, whom God has given to those who obey him.* (Acts 5:32 NIV)

46) The Spirit shares God's gifts.

> *If you then, though you are evil, know how to give good gifts to your children, how much more will your Father in heaven give the Holy Spirit to those who ask him!* (Luke 11:13 NIV)

47) The Spirit enables us to worship.

> *God is spirit, and his worshipers must worship in the Spirit and in truth.* (John 4:24 NIV)

48) The Spirit gives meaning to life.

> *The Spirit gives life; the flesh counts for nothing. The words I have spoken to you—they are full of the Spirit and life.* (John 6:63 NIV)

49) The Spirit brings forth service to others.

> *But now, by dying to what once bound us, we have been released from the law so that we serve in the new way of the Spirit, and not in the old way of the written code.* (Rom. 7:6 NIV)

50) The Spirit is with us to beckon Christ's return.

> *The Spirit and the bride say, "Come!" And let the one who hears say, "Come!" Let the one who is thirsty come; and let the one who wishes take the free gift of the water of life.* (Rev. 22:17 NIV)

LOVE MAKES THE WORLD GO 'ROUND

We've all heard the saying that "Love makes the world go 'round." But how fast? According to Astrosociety.org, our world spins counterclockwise at about 1,000 mph; the earth revolves around the sun at the rate of 66,000 mph; the movement of the sun/solar system within the Milky Way galaxy is 43,000 mph; while the orbit of the galaxy is rated at 483,000 mph; the movement of the galaxy in the universe is moving at the phenomenal rate of 1.3 million mph!

This galaxy, with you and me in it, is spinning in a vortex! It has been said that a picture is worth a thousand words, so we are sharing the picture below to help illustrate this point. It is obvious that this world will stand still for no one.

The movement of the earth is easy to see in time-lapse photography of the stars.

Conversely, "agape" love from God waits for everyone. Agape love is the perfect, unconditional love from God—perfect in the sense that God cannot love us any more or love us any less.

The following three examples represent agape love as expressed through the Trinity:

1. John 3:16 (KJV) tells us that "God so loved the world, that he gave His only begotten Son, that whosoever believeth in Him should not perish but have everlasting life." (To us, "whosoever" includes everyone.)

2. In Luke 23:34 (NIV), we see agape love is further exemplified by **Jesus** as He was being nailed to the cross. Jesus said, "Father, forgive them, for they do not know what they are doing." If giving up His life for us was not enough, asking for forgiveness for his murderers was further proof. (See the Four Steps of Forgiveness below.)

3. In John 14:17 (NIV, emphasis added), Jesus is speaking directly to the disciples about the Holy Spirit as the Spirit of truth, saying "The world cannot accept him, because it neither sees him nor knows him. But you know him, for He lives "WITH" you and will be "IN" you." This promise from Jesus of "will be IN you" indicates that the **Holy Spirit** would be residing in the disciples—which happened the moment of the blowing, violent wind in Acts 2:1–4, previously mentioned in the section about the Holy Spirit throughout history. (This promise from Jesus applies to our lives as it did the disciples' lives.)

DOES LOVE MAKE YOUR WORLD GO 'ROUND?

In the very first chapter of Genesis, we learned that we are made in God's image and likeness—yet, each of us is one-of-a-kind. David thanked God by saying in Psalm 139:13–16 (NLT), "you made all the delicate, inner parts of my body and knit me together in my mother's womb. Thank you for making me so wonderfully complex. Your workmanship is marvelous—how well I know it. You watched me as I was being formed in utter seclusion, as I was woven together in the dark of the womb. You saw me before I was born. Every day of my life was recorded in your book. Every moment was laid out before a single day had passed."

A movie about the creation process might give us a better understanding of God's love for us.

Would our attitudes change if you and I were allowed to watch a movie about the day we were created? Would we finally be able to understand the mystery of love if we were shown that there is no mystery at all? Would it change the way we think today if we could fully see and, more importantly, feel the impact of the agape love our Creator bestowed as every molecule and chromosome was being assembled and the moment His breath first filled our lungs?

What if the background music during the movie was, "Have Thine Own Way"? Written in 1907 by Adelaide Pollard, the lyrics still speak to us:

Have thine own way, Lord, Have thine own way,
Thou art the potter, I am the clay.
Mold me and make me after Thy will,
While I am waiting, yielded and still.

Would we change our attitudes about our own self-image? Would we forget about all the television commercials that tell us, "This is too small, and that is too large" or "That is too flat, or this is too round?" Would we feel differently about the Potter? Would we feel differently about the clay?

What if we noticed during the manufacturing of the heart that there was a switch installed on the top left corner of the heart labeled: "HS/FS"? We would naturally question the meaning of the switch. In this scenario, toward the end of the movie, the screen then reads: "Stand By." As we continue to watch, text scrolls on the screen to explain the following:

WE KNOW THAT YOU ARE QUESTIONING THE SWITCH THAT NEVER SHOWS UP ON X-RAYS BUT ONLY SHOWS UP ON OUR MOVIE. THE "HS/FS" IS A SWITCH INSTALLED EXCLUSIVELY FOR THE HOLY SPIRIT—HS. HE IS THE ONLY ONE WHO CAN ACTIVATE THE SWITCH AFTER HE IS LIVING INSIDE YOU. HE ONLY ENTERS UPON YOUR INVITATION.

THE "F" IS FOR FORGIVENESS, WHICH IS A FOUR-STEP PROCESS THAT WILL BE DESCRIBED TO YOU. AND THE "S" IS TO BE EXPLAINED AFTER YOU HAVE TAKEN THE FOUR STEPS OF FORGIVENESS.

The movie concludes with:

HAVE A NICE DAY!

BY THE WAY, WE HAVE DECIDED TO GIVE YOU ONE MORE DAY. WE WILL NOT REVEAL IF YOU HAVE ANY MORE DAYS AFTER THIS, SO WE SUGGEST THAT YOU MAKE THE MOST OF TODAY.

P.S. GET BUSY WITH THE FORGIVENESS AND ALWAYS REMEMBER THAT WE LOVE YOU.

PRODUCED BY: THE FATHER, THE SON, AND THE HOLY SPIRIT

TAKING FOUR STEPS OF FORGIVENESS

Get ready . . . the forgiveness model is going to require us to do some incredibly challenging work. Some of these steps could be the hardest work we have ever done. We may fall but do not worry, it will get easier; please keep trying. As we climb the steps, the work intensifies, but we must remember that the Holy Spirit will help us. We tell Him about our pain, and He will bless us with our gain. Ephesians 4:31–32 (NIV) reads, "Get rid of all bitterness, rage and anger, brawling and slander, along with every form of malice. Be kind and compassionate to one another, forgiving each other, just as in Christ God forgave you."

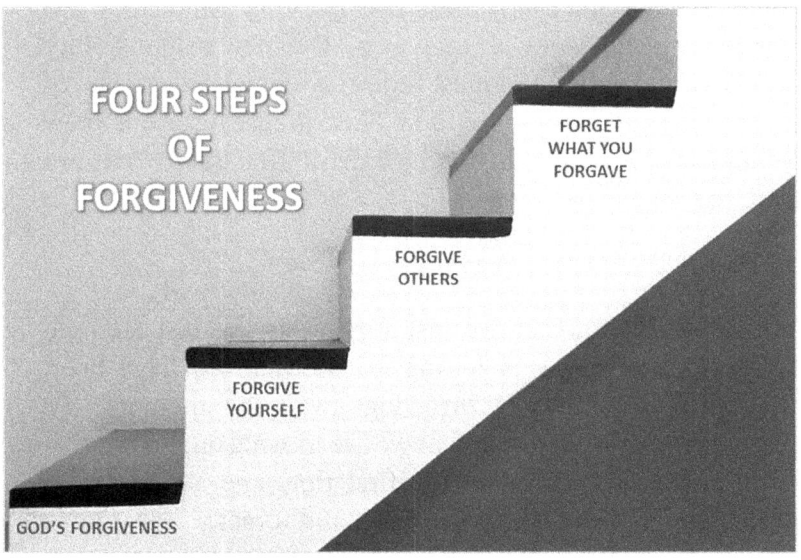

Taking four steps of forgiveness can lead to inner peace.

Step 1. Seek God's Forgiveness

We have to ask for our own forgiveness first. Cleansing and purging softens our hearts and opens the path for God's Holy Spirit. The minute that we doubt or take time to question whether God can forgive certain sins, we should stop. We cannot judge what God will or will not forgive before we confess that we are powerless to control our lives. Just try it.

Step 2. Forgive Ourselves

Forgiving ourselves is the next step. Forgiving ourselves is a continuation of the purging that began in Step 1. We have to forgive ourselves because Christ paid the price for our sins, and we are forgiven. There are no exceptions to Step 2. Read Step 1 again for clarity.

Step 3. Forgive Others

Forgiving those who have hurt us is next. Our friends and family can often hurt us the most since they are closest to us emotionally. They may not ask for forgiveness because they think they are entitled to say or do whatever they want. Our new responsibility is to forgive them with no request required—which can be one of the most difficult things we do. This is because our new forgiveness is the reflection in the mirror that says, "We are forgiven, so we have to forgive."

Step 4. Forget That Which We Forgave

Forgetting everything that we just forgave is the last step we climb. Since forgiveness is letting go of what we have been holding onto, forgetting is throwing away the memory. To eliminate the memory is to say that we are moving on; taking this step is a true accomplishment the first time and a way of life thereafter. For your sake, let go, forgive, and forget.

ACTIVATING THE SWITCH MARKED "S"

The letter "S" stands for servant or serve. In Matthew 20:28 (NIV), Jesus himself said that "He did not come to be served, but to serve." We were not created just to consume resources—watch TV, eat popcorn, and accumulate more "stuff." We have all heard the saying that "you can't take it with you," but you can take the memory of making a difference in someone else's life.

YOUR STORY IS WAITING TO BE WRITTEN

Serving others is fun if you choose something that uses the talents with which you are blessed. First Peter 4:10 tells us that we should use the gifts we have received to serve others. The gifts that God has given you are as unique as your fingerprints. Think about your natural skills, and ask God to show you how He wants you to use them. You can start small and maybe serve by speaking a kind word to someone who needs it; opening the door for someone with arms full of groceries; or donating old shoes, clothing, or household items to charity.

Or perhaps there is a community center near you full of elementary children enrolled in a reading assistance program requiring volunteers. Now you say, "That just isn't for me because I am not **comfortable** working with kids." Fine, there are 45,000,000 seniors over the age of sixty-five in the United States. There are programs in your local communities for the specific purpose of assisting seniors, and you can use Google to find out which senior agencies are located near you and how to volunteer. Maybe you could rake leaves for a widow who has back trouble and is on the list of those needing help. Now you say, "But I am not **comfortable** working with seniors." Fine, there are over 450,000 churches in the United States, and I am sure that something needs to be repaired, painted, swept, cleaned, or organized. Many churches rely on "trustees" who are volunteers in the church to do this work. Walk in the church office and ask the volunteer who greeted you to talk with you about volunteering your services. Now you say, "But I am not **comfortable** walking in a church—they don't even know me in there. By introducing yourself and offering your help, you will meet new people. If you like working with food, a homeless shelter in your community might appreciate volunteers to help feed the homeless. In our area, you can walk through their door and introduce yourself and be contributing within minutes. There is always food to cook, serve, or clean up. If they ask you who sent you, tell them God did. So you say, "But I am an atheist, and I am not **comfortable** saying the name God." FINE, THEN TELL THEM SOME IDIOT FROM THE VORTEX SENT YOU! Just try something; anything that stretches you can make you more than you were. Try one of the suggestions above and observe how it makes you feel when you reach out. If you notice someone without a smile, then give them yours.

So don't walk away—run away from your comfort zone. We are all human and creatures of habit with a tendency to live in our comfort zones. But as this book started with a prayer encouraging us to see the needs of others and do something to help, we end it with the same idea. Stepping outside your comfort zone can open the door to serving and making a difference in other people's lives. Our prayer is that you will join us and millions of others who volunteer their services to benefit others every day.

We'll see you in the Vortex!

VORTEX ACKNOWLEDGEMENTS

The events that happened and this story would not have been possible without the incredible encouragement, support, and love of many people. This list below includes some of the people who had a role before, during, or after Superstorm Sandy. Each of you has my heartfelt and enduring gratitude.

Susan: you are the greatest gift from God! I can't be more thankful or excited about the "yoke" that we share. You always go the extra mile for anyone who asks you for anything. You have gone the extra Galaxy for me—at the earlier referenced speed of 483,000 mph. This book would never have been written or experienced without you. Your relentless dedication to the editing, imagery, tone, art, diction, and inflection of this text was your very best. While your opinion was not always what I wanted to hear, it was rooted in truth and delivered in love. Our many talks at 2:00 or 3:00 a.m. also served as part of the foundation of work that went into this incredible story. Your passion and love for music is evidenced by your 5:00 a.m. singing in the shower, which is such a blessing. Your gentle care and love for all living creatures is an example we could all learn from. Thank you for reminding me of why in all things, I should give thanks. I love you.

Charlotte: nothing about this story could have happened without you opening your door and, more importantly, opening your heart. I knew the moment that I introduced myself to you and you hugged me (instead of shooting me) that I was in the right place. You, Roy, and Ryan immediately went to work to make people aware of our food, and we saw hurt and sadness transformed to laughter and fun. We experienced everything from elation to exhaustion and back again. You worked constantly and never complained one time, proving that serving others is in your blood. Thank you for letting me stay with you the entire first week. You will always remain the Matriarch of Little

Ferry to me, and your driveway will always contain a piece of my heart. Matthew 7:7–8 (NIV) says to ask, seek, and knock: "Ask and it will be given to you; seek and you will find; knock and the door will be opened to you. For everyone who asks receives; the one who seeks finds; and to the one who knocks, the door will be opened." The sequence of these verses occurred exactly as written. We love you all, and I can't thank you enough.

Roy: thank you for serving and for your part in our collective effort to help others after the storm. I have fond memories of the shorts you modeled and your efforts to make a country boy speak "Joisey." You were kind to everyone who filled your driveway and played a crucial part in the collective success we all experienced. Thank you.

Ryan: you were always there and coordinated people coming and going with precision. You were constantly on the phone, and I suppose the word Samsung is embossed on your ear. We laughed and had fun, and we had our softer moments as well. You are more of a brother than a great friend. I know you will continue to lead those kids on the football field that bears your own grandfather's name. He would be so proud to see his legacy carried on. Your greatest asset is that you show servant leadership in the lives of the guys on the team and, more importantly, you don't want any credit for that. You will never take any money with you from this life, but the difference you made in the lives of those kids, you will. Thank you for making my time with you so special.

Mayor Mauro Raguseo, Little Ferry, New Jersey: you were the caring Father of Little Ferry when hearts were hurting and damage was everywhere. When we first met, you were so concerned about everyone and that never changed. I remember that you knew stories about hundreds of people while your own home was filled with water. Your home was the least of your worries, and everyone else's problems dominated your conversation. Your dedication that I observed should have been

ACKNOWLEDGEMENTS

videotaped. Thank you for your care, your concern, and your incredible model of servant leadership.

Joe and Lisa: you guys were an incredible team. Lisa, you always seemed to be there when I needed you. That was a great feeling. Your hot shower was a welcome gift while others had no electricity. Opening your home to Blaine, Jonathan, and me for trip number two was amazing. We all had so much fun. Thank you for feeding us and hundreds of others. Your service was appreciated by everyone. Joe, you were a blessing to so many people with your relentless hours of cooking. This was such an incredible gift you gave of yourself. Several back up volunteers were ready to take over when you needed a break—I just don't remember you taking one. Your service to others is the very heart of what we are all called to do. Your careful count of meat in the cooler gave us accuracy on knowing how many people were fed. I so appreciate everything you did to make the trip so special.

Blaine and Jonathan: thank you both for hearing the call and going on trip number two. Jonathan, your respect for your mother and dad is a model that I would like to show others. I would take eight ounces of your energy every day if I could. Thank you for allowing me to be a kid again. Your dad and I hoped that you would learn from this important experience and share your passion for serving others. Blaine, your willingness to drive probably saved my life. From the Donut Bank Bible Studies to the reality of serving in the field, you prove that you are well suited for all of it. Thank you for allowing Susan and me to become a part of your family.

Frank J.: you have spent your life saving the lives of others, and now, your son follows the same path. Thank you for your input on the book and the technical stuff that firemen know. I am honored to be your friend. Thank you for every single life that you have touched in your career and beyond. You are a true servant.

Frank: my experience took a different turn the moment that you asked me to go with you on the emergency run. It was nothing short of the ride of a lifetime. I love my "honorary membership" in the Little Ferry Fire Department, and the LFFD glasses are safely sitting in a cabinet behind glass doors. I am in awe of your service to others, and that really defines the true meaning of this book. The difference is: I had to be awakened to act; you volunteer to act, give, and live the experience every day. Thank you for your friendship.

Gary D.: since I am taking my hat off to the firemen, I thank you as well. You have made me feel like a part of the firemen family. Thanks for all you have done and all you do in the service of others. I have laughed at some of the most unique images and videos that you post on Facebook.

Joe, Robin, Mia, and Massimo: you are another fireman's family that I honor, respect, and see on Facebook. Thanks, guys, for being there every day and being part of everything. The kids were such a refreshing break from all the other activities. I love you all.

Cindy and the triplets: Cindy, thank you for coming over each day and bringing the kids. Their three little hugs melted my heart. I am glad that we can keep up with all the activities through Facebook. You are a wonderful mother and teacher. Thank you again.

Marty and Patty: thank you for opening your home and hospitality to me while I was in Little Ferry. Patty, you worked the phone as you wanted the story to be seen by others. You were part of every day and your support is so appreciated. Thank you.

Kenney, Pauley, and Alby: guys, you were terrific in that driveway. I never had to look far to find any of you. Pauley, your presidential trivia is absolutely awesome and could serve as stand up entertainment any time. Kenney, it looks like you replaced New Jersey ice and snow with the Palm Trees in Florida. Congrats to you guys. Alby, you were such a regular for us, and we enjoyed your help and pitching in when you could. Not many people look

ACKNOWLEDGEMENTS

forward to becoming a homeowner and have the foundation and walls up and are greeted by the monster that Sandy was. You still came over to help us while the new house got rebuilt, and we appreciated everything. Thanks to all of you guys for helping make it such an incredible operation.

Pastor Steve and Jayna Beutler, Methodist Temple, Evansville, Indiana: your loving friendship and encouragement are only exceeded by your quintessential examples of humility. Jayna, how right you were to recognize that the strength of a mission is dependent upon the strength of a marriage. Thank you both.

Pastor Jeff and Julie Buck, Mt. Auburn United Methodist Church, Greenwood, Indiana: we are so blessed for your roles before, during, and after the trips. Your love has never changed by time or distance apart. You were always there when I needed you. Thank you.

Pastor Chris and Dolli Neikirk, Hillside United Methodist Church, Princeton, Indiana: your encouragement and love jump-started us out of the comfort zone, but we didn't realize at the time that it would be permanent. Thank you for your contribution to the beginning to this story and subsequent trips to your office.

Reverend Beth Whalley Mitchell, Tenafly United Methodist Church, Tenafly, New Jersey: the hospitality and kindness shown to me for the two consecutive Sundays that I attended your services were great. You said, "Isn't it amazing that no matter which state you are in, once you are in a United Methodist Church, you always feel at home?" I did and have you to thank for that.

Pastor Carl and Merlene Mann, New Horizon Fellowship Church, Evansville, Indiana: Pastor Carl, thank you for your discerning and caring attention given to me after returning from my first trip to New Jersey. When I called you the first time, it was as though you already knew that I needed to speak with you.

I couldn't discuss the spiritual experience from the carnality perspective with anyone but you. You revealed that I needed to find my way to the center of the vortex. The second phone call was to tell you about the Voice at 2:00 every morning, encouraging this book. Your cautionary response, "If you decide that you are going to write, make sure that you tell the entire story. If you leave anything unsaid, you may always regret it," stayed in my head for the last two years. I am confident in saying that that one single statement was a light that illuminated the path for completing this task. Susan and I love you both. Thank you.

Tom and Janet, Dewig Meats: we are so appreciative of your contributions to our outreach efforts. You have touched people in so many ways when their world was torn apart and for many, still is. Thank you for your generous donations. You both have servants' hearts.

Bruce and Anne: our response to disasters started behind your house in a barn and a driveway full of cars. I remember many nights that Anne said, "I am going to bed and I'm leaving it with you guys." It was the sleet hitting us in the face when the shower trailers had to be moved out of the barn and into the driveway that made it so special. And the second trailer was the total leap of faith. Thank you both for stretching us beyond our wildest dreams and energizing such a great group of people for the concept, construction, and delivery of not one, but two shower trailers to Gulfport, Mississippi. You guys are so special to us and always will be. Thank you.

Laura: you may have moved to California, but your spirit is still all Hoosier. Thank you for the time you invested in reading a very early draft of the book. Your feedback was taken to heart. We knew your comments were guided from the Center of the vortex. Thank you again.

Aunt June: your faith and devotion to the Lord are so inspiring. Not everyone eighty-five years young can quote the things they learned as a child in a St. Lucas Sunday School class. Thank you

ACKNOWLEDGEMENTS

for the helpful feedback on an early version of the book as well as your incredible enthusiasm supporting Susan and me in our continued outreach.

Dr. Cathy W.: we are so appreciative of the time that you took for the review of an early version of the book. Your insightful comments stimulated deeper thinking. We have had such great communication as the Parakletos had fun with the three of us. We respect your input and your friendship. Thank you. We are praying that you reach the vertex of your vortex!

Garry and Mavis: thank you for your encouragement and support. Mavis, your incredible insight and pastoral upbringing was always a lighthouse in the fog. We will always call you family. Thank you for being there and staying in our corner.

Donut Bank Brothers—Chad, Jeff, and Joe: guys, you were there for every page that turned in front of me. Your encouragement and foundation provided so much support as I struggled to understand the meaning of everything. You each contributed the following points that stand out in my mind as I look at the last five years of meeting at 6:00 a.m. at the Donut Bank:

Joe, I like your saying: "There are people born on third base and wake up with the thought: Wow, I hit a triple." After months of pondering, I finally get it.

Jeff, your math equation of the relationship between maturity, obedience, and knowledge is great. We know that obedience is the driving factor for spiritual maturity.

$$\text{Spiritual Maturity} = \frac{\text{Obedience}}{\text{Knowledge}}$$

Chad, your instruction to pull out every dictionary and mark through the word "coincidence" is exactly what I did. Everything happens for a reason, and there are no accidents. I have used that statement so many times. Thank you, guys, for your incredible support over the years.

Evansville Tri-State Tres Dias Community: thank you for providing locally, nationally, and internationally, the living example of Psalm 119:105 (NIV): Thy word is a lamp unto my feet and a light unto my path. Everyone should be encouraged to participate in this three-day weekend during which you leave the world behind and soak in God's love expressed through the body of Christ. Some of the most powerful experiences involve the men who walk in with needle marks on their arms but walk out with crosses around their necks, a glow upon their faces, and a burning passion to tell a new story about their lives.

Pastor Dan Kennedy: your leadership during a Tres Dias weekend is something I will never forget. You were the living embodiment of the armor of God, with a shield of faith and the sword of the Spirit. Thank you for your example.

Our Methodist Temple and Blue Grass UMC friends who donated funds toward the expenses of the trip: you lifted spirits and sent hugs that I can safely say were personally delivered. Thank you for helping make everything possible.

COMING SOON

**Vortex of the Holy Spirit
Study Guide**

**Fifty Functions of the Holy Spirit
And How They Apply to Your Everyday Life**

The events following Superstorm Sandy caused many changes in our lives. Find out what's happening now at
www.VortexMinistries.com

Contact us:

david@vortexministries.com
susan@vortexministries.com

Like us on Facebook:

https://www.facebook.com/VortexMinistries

www.ingramcontent.com/pod-product-compliance
Lightning Source LLC
Chambersburg PA
CBHW071710090426
42738CB00009B/1727